Retrotopia

To Aleksandra, companion of my thought and life

Retrotopia

Zygmunt Bauman

polity

First published in 2017 by Polity Press

10

Polity Press
65 Bridge Street
Cambridge CB2 1UR, UK

Polity Press
350 Main Street
Malden, MA 02148, USA

ISBN-13: 978-1-5095-1531-8
ISBN-13: 978-1-5095-1532-5 (pb)

A catalogue record for this book is available from the British Library.

Library of Congress Cataloging-in-Publication Data

Names: Bauman, Zygmunt, 1925- author.
Title: Retrotopia / Zygmunt Bauman.
Description: Malden, MA : Polity, 2017. | Includes bibliographical references and index.
Identifiers: LCCN 2016029145 (print) | LCCN 2016058070 (ebook) | ISBN 9781509515318 (hardback) | ISBN 9781509515325 (paperback) | ISBN 9781509515332 (EPdf) | ISBN 9781509515349 (Mobi) | ISBN 9781509515356 (Epub)
Subjects: LCSH: Utopias--History--21st century. | Social action. | BISAC: SOCIAL SCIENCE / Sociology / General.
Classification: LCC HX806 .B278 2017 (print) | LCC HX806 (ebook) | DDC 335/.02--dc23
LC record available at https://lccn.loc.gov/2016029145

Typeset in 11 on 14 pt Sabon by
Servis Filmsetting Ltd, Stockport, Cheshire
Printed and bound in Great Britain by TJ Books Limited, Padstow

For further information on Polity, visit our website:
politybooks.com

Contents

Introduction:
The Age of Nostalgia

This (in case you have forgotten) is what Walter Benjamin had to say in his 'Theses on the Philosophy of History' written in the early 1940s about the message conveyed by the Angelus Novus (renamed the 'Angel of History') – drawn by Paul Klee in 1920:

> The face of the angel of history is turned toward the past. Where we perceived a chain of events, he sees a single catastrophe which keeps piling wreckage and hurls it in front of his feet. The angel would like to stay, awaken the dead, and make whole what has been smashed. But a storm is blowing from Paradise; it has got caught in his wings with such violence that the angel can no longer close them. This storm irresistably propels him into the future to which his back is turned, while the pile of debris before him grows skyward. The storm is what we call progress.

Were one to look closely at Klee's drawing almost a century after Benjamin put on record his unfathomably profound and indeed incomparable insight, one would catch the Angel of History once more in full flight. What might, however, strike the viewer most, is the Angel changing direction – the Angel of History caught in the midst of a U-turn: his face turning from the past to the future, his wings being pushed backwards by the storm blowing this time from the imagined, anticipated and feared in advance Hell of the future towards the Paradise of the past (as, probably, it is retrospectively imagined after it has been lost and fallen into ruins) – though the wings are pressed now, as they were pressed then, with such mighty violence 'that the angel can no longer close them'.

Past and future, one may conclude, are in that drawing captured in the course of exchanging their respective virtues and vices, listed – as suggested by Benjamin – 100 years ago by Klee. It is now the future, whose time to be pillorized seems to have arrived after being first decried for its untrustworthiness and unmanageability, that is booked on the debit side. And it is now the past's turn to be booked on the side of credit – a credit deserved (whether genuinely or putatively) by a site of still-free choice and investment of still-undiscredited hope.

*

Nostalgia – as Svetlana Boym, Harvard Professor of Slavic and Comparative Literature, suggests[1] – 'is a sentiment of loss and displacement, but it is also a romance with one's own fantasy' (p. xiii). While in the seventeenth century nostalgia was treated as an eminently curable disease, which Swiss doctors, for instance, recommended could be cured with opium, leeches and a trip to the mountains, 'by the twenty-first century the passing ailment turned into the incurable modern condition. The twentieth century began with a futuristic utopia and ended with nostalgia' (p. xiv). Boym concludes by diagnosing the present-day 'global epidemic of nostalgia, an affective yearning for a community with a collective memory, a longing for continuity in a fragmented world' – and proposes to view that epidemic as 'a defence mechanism in a time of accelerated rhythms of life and historical upheavals' (ibid.). That 'defensive mechanism' consists essentially in 'the promise to rebuild the ideal home that lies at the core of many powerful ideologies of today, tempting us to relinquish critical thinking for emotional bonding'. And she warns: 'The danger of nostalgia is that it tends to confuse the actual home and the imaginary one' (p. xvi). Finally, she offers a hint where to seek, and most likely find, such dangers: in the 'restorative' variety of nostalgia – one characteristic of 'national and nationalist revivals all over the world, which engage in the antimodern myth-making of history by means of a return to national symbols and myths and, occasionally, through swapping conspiracy theories' (p. 41).

Let me observe that nostalgia is but one member of the rather extended family of affectionate relationship with an 'elsewhere'. This sort of affection (and so, by proxy, all the temptations and traps Boym spotted in the current 'global epidemic of nostalgia') have been endemic and un-detachable ingredients of the human condition since at least the – difficult to pinpoint exactly – moment of discovery of the *optionality* of human choices; or – more precisely – they are such since the discovery that human conduct is, and cannot but be, a matter of choice, and (by the all-but-natural contrivance of projection) that the world here and now is but one of the un-definable number of possible worlds – past, present and future. The 'global epidemic of nostalgia' took over the baton from the (gradually yet unstoppably globalizing) 'epidemic of progress frenzy' in the relay race of history.

The chase, however, goes on, uninterrupted. It might change direction, even the racecourse – but it won't stop. Kafka attempted to captivate in words that inner, inextinguishable and insatiable imperative that commands us – and probably will continue to do so till Hell freezes over:

> I heard the sound of a trumpet, and I asked my servant what it meant. He knew nothing and had heard nothing. At the gate he stopped me and asked: 'Where is the master going?' 'I don't know,' I said, 'just out of here, just out of here. Out of here, nothing else, it's the only way I can reach my goal.' 'So you know your goal?' he asked. 'Yes,' I replied, 'I've just told you. Out of here – that is my goal.'[2]

*

Five hundred years after Thomas More put the name of 'Utopia' on the millennia-long human dream of return to Paradise or establishing Heaven on Earth, one more Hegelian triad formed by a double negation is presently nearing the completion of its full circle. After the prospects of human happiness – tied since More to a *topos* (a fixed place, a polis, a city, a sovereign state – each under a wise and benevolent ruler) – have been unfixed, untied from any particular *topos* and individualized, privatized and personalized ('subsidiarized' to human individuals after the pattern of snails' homes), it is their turn now to be negated by what they valiantly and all but successfully attempted to negate. From that double negation of More-style utopia – its rejection succeeded by resurrection – 'retrotopias' are currently emerging: visions located in the lost/stolen/abandoned but undead past, instead of being tied to the not-yet-unborn and so inexistent future, as was their twice-removed forebear:

> According to the Irish poet Oscar Wilde, upon reaching the Land of Plenty, we should once more fix our gaze on the farthest horizon and re-hoist the sails. 'Progress is the realization of Utopias', he wrote. But the far horizon's a blank. The Land of Plenty is banked in fog. Precisely when we should be shouldering the historic task of investing this rich, safe, and healthy existence with meaning, we've buried utopia instead. There's no new dream to replace it because we can't imagine a better world than the one we've got. In fact, most parents in wealthy countries believe their children will actually be *worse* off – from 53 percent of parents in Australia to 90 percent in France. Parents in wealthy countries expect their children will be worse off than they (as a percentage).

So notes Rutger Bregman in his most recent, 2016 book *Utopia for Realists* (subtitled *The Case for a Universal Basic Income, Open Borders, and a 15–hour Workweek*).

Privatization/individualization of the idea of 'progress' and of the pursuit of life's improvements were sold by the powers that be and embraced by most of their subjects as liberation: breaking free from the stern demands of subordination and discipline – at the cost of social services and state protection. For a great and growing number of subjects, such liberation proved, slowly yet consistently, to be a mixed blessing – or even a blessing adulterated by a considerable and still swelling admixture of curse.

Annoyances of constraints were replaced with no less demeaning, frightening and aggravating risks that can't but saturate the condition of self-reliance by decree. The fear of non-contribution/corrections supplied by the conformity of yore, its immediate predecessor, was replaced by a no less agonizing horror of inadequacy. As the old fears drifted gradually into oblivion and the new ones gained in volume and intensity, promotion and degradation, progress and retrogression changed places – at least for a growing number of unwilling pawns in the game, they were – or felt themselves to be – doomed to defeat. This prompted the pendulums of the public mindset and mentality to perform a U-turn: from investing public hopes of improvement in the uncertain and ever-too-obviously un-trustworthy future, to re-reinvesting them in the vaguely remembered past, valued for its assumed stability and so trustworthiness. With such a U-turn happening, the future is transformed from the natural habitat of hopes and rightful expectations into the site of nightmares: horrors of losing your job together with its attached social standing, of having your home together with the rest of life's goods and chattels 'repossessed', of helplessly watching your children sliding down the well-being-cum-prestige slope and your own laboriously learned and memorized skills stripped of whatever has been left of their market value. The road to future turns looks uncannily as a trail of corruption and degeneration. Perhaps the road back, to the past, won't miss the chance of turning into a trail of cleansing from the damages committed by futures, whenever they turned into a present?

The impact of such a shift, as I'll argue in this book, is visible and palpably felt *at every level* of social cohabitation – in its emergent worldview and the life-strategies that this worldview insinuates and gestates. Javier Solana's latest diagnosis of the form that impact assumes[3] at the level of the European Union – (an avant-garde experiment in raising national integration to a supra-national level) – may, with but relatively minor adjustment, serve as an X-ray image of the back-to-the-past turn observable at all other levels. Different levels deploy different languages, but use them to convey strikingly similar stories.

As Solana puts it, 'The European Union has a dangerous case of nostalgia. Not only is a yearning for the 'good old days' – before the EU supposedly impinged on national sovereignty – fuelling the rise of nationalist political parties; European leaders continue to try to apply yesterday's solutions to today's problems.' And he explains why it has happened, drawing his argument from the most recent, most drastic and most attention-drawing departures –

> In the wake of the 2008 global financial crisis, the EU's weaker economies faced skyrocketing unemployment, especially among young people, while its stronger economies felt pressure to 'show solidarity' by bailing out countries in distress. When the stronger economies provided those bailouts, they included demands for austerity that impeded the recipients' economic recovery. Few were satisfied, and many blamed European integration.

– only to warn, that taking such charge at its face-value is a fatal mistake threatening to draw us away from the only way to sanitize the present plight that may be justifiably sought and hopefully found:

While the economic pain that many Europeans feel is certainly real, the nationalists' diagnosis of its source is false. The reality is that the EU can be criticized for *the way it handled the crisis*; but it cannot be blamed for the global economic imbalances that have fuelled economic strife since 2008. Those imbalances reflect a much broader phenomenon: globalization. Some have used disenchanting experiences with globalization as an excuse for a return to protectionism and the supposedly halcyon days of strong national borders. Others, wistfully recalling a nation-state that never really existed, cling to national sovereignty as a reason to refuse further European integration. Both groups question the foundations of the European project. But their memory fails them, and their yearnings mislead them.

*

What I call 'retrotopia', is a derivative of the aforementioned second degree of negation – negation of utopia's negation, one that shares with Thomas More's legacy its fixity on a territorially sovereign *topos*: a firm ground thought to provide, and hopefully guarantee, an acceptable modicum of stability and therefore a satisfactory degree of self-assurance. It differs, however, from that legacy in approving, absorbing and incorporating the contributions/corrections supplied by its immediate predecessor: namely, the replacement of the 'ultimate perfection' idea with the assumption of the non-finality and endemic dynamism of the order it promotes, allowing thereby for the possibility (as well as desirability) of an indefinite succession of further changes that such an idea *a priori* de-legitimizes and precludes. True to the utopian spirit, retrotopia derives its stimulus from the hope of reconciling, at long last, *security* with *freedom*:

the feat that both the original vision and its first negation didn't try – or, having attempted, failed – to attain.

I intend to follow this brief sketch of the most notable
meanders of the post-More, 500–years-long history of
modern utopia, with an exercise in unravelling, portraying and putting on record some of the most remarkable
'back to the future' tendencies inside the emergent 'retrotopian' phase in utopia's history – in particular,
rehabilitation of the tribal model of community, return
to the concept of a primordial/pristine self predeter-
mined by non-cultural and culture-immune factors, and
all in all retreat from the presently held (prevalent in
both social science and popular opinions) view of the
essential, presumably non-negotiable and *sine qua non*
features of the 'civilized order'.

These three departures do not of course signal a
straightforward return to a previously practised mode of
life – since this would be, as Ernest Gellner convincingly
argued, a sheer impossibility. They are rather (to deploy
Derrida's conceptual distinction) conscious attempts at
iteration, rather than *reiteration*, of the *status quo ante*,
existing or imagined to have been existing before the
second negation – its image having been by now significantly recycled and modified anyway, in the process of
selective memorizing, intertwined with selective forget-
ting. All the same, it is the genuine or putative aspects
of the past, believed to be successfully tested and unduly
abandoned or recklessly allowed to erode, that serve as
main orientation/reference points in drawing the road-
map to Retrotopia.

To put the retrotopian romance with the past into
the right perspective, one more caveat is – from the very
start – in order. Boym suggests that a nostalgia epidemic

'often follows revolutions' – adding wisely that in the case of the 1789 French Revolution it was 'not only the *ancien régime* that produced revolution, but in some respect the revolution produced the ancien régime, giving it a shape, a sense of closure and a gilded aura', whereas it was the fall of Communism that gave birth to an image of the last Soviet decades as a 'golden age of stability, strength and "normalcy", the view prevalent in Russia today'.[4] In other words: what we as a rule 'return to' when dreaming our nostalgic dreams is not the past 'as such' – not the past 'wie es ist eigentlich gewesen' ('as it genuinely was'), which Leopold von Ranke advised historians to recover and represent (and many a historian, though with well short of unanimous acclaim, earnestly tried). We can read in E. H. Carr's highly influential *What is History?*:[5]

> the historian is necessarily selective. The belief in a hard core of historical facts existing objectively and independently of the historian is a preposterous fallacy, but one which it is very hard to eradicate . . . It used to be said that the facts speak for themselves. This is, of course, untrue. The facts speak only when the historian calls on them: it is he who decides to which facts to give the floor, and in what order of context.[6]

Carr addressed his argument to his fellow professional historians, to whom he granted the earnest desire to find and convey truth, the whole truth, and only the truth. In 1961, when the first copies of *What is History?* appeared on bookshelves, the widespread use, indeed the commonality of the 'politics of memory' – a code-name for the practice of an arbitrary selection and/or discarding of facts for political (in fact partisan) purposes – was not, however, as yet a public secret as it has become now, thanks in large part to George Orwell's alarming, blood-curdling vivisection of the 'Ministry of Truth' continuously 'updating' (rewriting) historical records to catch up with the fast-changing state policies. Whatever road the professional seekers of historical truth have chosen to pursue, and however hard they might have tried to hold to the choice they made, their findings and their voices are not the only ones accessible on the public forum. Neither are they necessarily the most audible among competing voices, nor guaranteed to reach the widest audience – whereas their most resourceful competitors and most unscrupulous inspectors and managers tend to put pragmatic utility above the truth of the matter as the prime criterion in setting their right narrations apart from the wrong.

There are good reasons to surmise that the advent of the world-wide web and the Internet signals the decline of Ministries of Truth (though by no means the twilight of the 'politics of historical memory'; if anything, it expanded the opportunities for this to be conducted, while making its instruments accessible more widely than ever before and its impacts potentially more intense and consequential – even if not more durable). The demise of the Ministries of Truth (that is, of an unchallenged monopoly by the powers-that-be on passing verdicts on truthfulness) hasn't, however, smoothed the path for the messages sent by the professional seekers and articulators of the 'truth of the matter' to public consciousness; if anything, this made that road yet more cluttered, twisted, treacherous and wobbly.

*

Following the deepening gap between power and politics – that is, the ability to have things done and the capability of deciding what things need to be done, once vested with the territorially sovereign state – the original idea of pursuing human happiness through the design-and-build of a society more hospitable to human needs, dreams and cravings came to be seen as increasingly nebulous for the lack of an agency deemed fit to face up to the grandiosity of such a task and tackle the challenge of its awesome complexity. As Peter Drucker bluntly put it[7] (perhaps inspired in part by Margaret Thatcher's TINA – 'There Is No Alternative' – maxim), a society that once and for all links individual to social perfection is no longer on the cards, and there is no point in expecting salvation to come from society. And, as Ulrich Beck was shortly to spell it out, what followed was that it was now up to each human individual to seek and find or construe individual solutions to socially produced problems and apply them – while deploying one's own wit and individually possessed skills and resources. The target was no longer a better *society* (as making it better has for all practical intents and reasons become hopeless) – but improving one's own individual *position* inside that essentially and definitely incorrigible society. Instead of shared rewards for the collective efforts at social reform, there were individually appropriated spoils of competition.

*

My intention is to compose in the chapters that follow a preliminary inventory of the most spectacular, and perhaps also most seminal, departures linked to the advent of retrotopian sentiments and practices.

I
Back to Hobbes?

The suggestion that the question in the title is a mark of our times one can glean at any rate when perusing a recently fast-rising number of prognoses (some among them dressed/disguised as diagnoses), extrapolating, as is the way with predictions, from the most recent and statistically most common headlines. Hobbes' Leviathan – until not so long ago believed to have duly acquitted itself of its postulated mission of suppressing the inborn cruelty of humans, so making human life among humans liveable, and not 'nasty, brutish and short' as it would otherwise have been – is less and less trusted to do its job properly, or indeed to be capable of having its job properly done. Human endemic aggressiveness, resulting time and again in a propensity for violence, appears to have been anything but mitigated, let alone extinguished; it is very much alive and always ready to be kicking at a moment's notice – or indeed without notice.

The 'civilizing process' that was meant to have been designed, conducted and monitored by the modern state, looks more and more as Norbert Elias (whether intentionally or inadvertently) presented it: as a reform of human *manners*, not human *capacities, predispositions and impulses*. In the course of the civilizing process, acts of human violence were shuffled out of *sight*, not out of *human nature*, as well as 'outsourced', 'contracted out' to professionals (bespoke tailors, so to speak, of violence), or 'subsidiarized' to lesser, 'unclean' humans – e.g. slaves, bondage demi-slaves or servants (scapegoats, so to speak, on whose shoulders shameful sins of untamed aggression were dumped): a process not substantially different from that accomplished in India, many centuries before, by its caste system, which relegated the jobs considered impure, demeaning and polluting (such as, for instance, butchering, removal of rubbish, disposal of animal carcasses and of human waste) to the 'untouchables' – a caste outside the caste system: to the so-called 'Panchama' – the fifth caste, placed, without the right to return, outside (read: 'beneath'), or, more to the point, in a social void, stripped of the moral/behavioural rules binding, and by and large observed, inside the society proper – the four-partite Varna, to which the main bulk of Indian society was assumed to belong, just like their quite recent reincarnation in the form of the 'underclass' – a class outside the class system and so outside class-divided society. The 'civilizing' function of the 'civilizing process' consisted in putting paid to public executions, pillories or gallows on public squares, as well as shifting the job of quartering the blood-dripping animal carcasses from the dining rooms, where they'd be consumed, to the kitchens, seldom if ever visited by the diners; or, for that matter, in celebrating simultaneously the human natural mastery and contrived moral superiority over animals in the annual ritual of fox-hunting. Ervin Goffman would add to that list of civilizing jobs 'civil inattention' – the art of averting one's eyes from a stranger on the sidewalk, inside the shared carriage or in a dentist's waiting room – which signals an intention to abstain from engagement, lest an interaction between mutually unfamiliar actors lead to unsavoury impulses escaping control, and so to embarrassing disclosure of the 'animal in man' who needs be kept in a cage, under lock and key and out of sight.

With the help of these and similar stratagems and expedients, the Hobbesian animal inside the human emerged from the modern reform of manners untamed and intact, in its pristine and potent, crude, coarse, boorish/loutish form, which the civilizing process managed to veneer over and/or 'outsource' (as in the case of transferring displays of aggression from battlefields to football pitches), but not to mend, let alone to exorcise. That animal lies in waiting, ready to wipe out the dreadfully thin coating of conventional decorum – meant to hide the unprepossessing, rather than suppress and contain the sinister and gory.

Timothy Snyder suggests, in his re-reading and re-evaluating of the grisly and baneful experience of the Holocaust (and in particular of the fact of the evil being perpetrated by many, as the 'moral instinct' and 'human goodness' few only could afford and demonstrate):

> Perhaps we imagine that we would be rescuers in some future catastrophe. Yet if states were destroyed, local institutions corrupted, and economic incentives directed towards murder, few of us would behave well. There is little reason to think that we are ethically superior to the

Europeans of 1930s and 1940s, or for that matter less vulnerable to the kind of ideas that Hitler so successfully promulgated and realized.[1]

What we deemed, self-consolingly, to be (at least in its intention, if not in the already tangible effects) a social-engineering feat of excising and banishing Mr Hyde from Dr Jekyll's innards once and for all, looks and feels more and more like another Dorian Gray-style attempt at a cosmetic surgery designed to change places between reality and its presentation. If applied in real life, cosmetic interventions tend to require regular repetitions, as the effects of each one have, as a rule, a short life-expectancy. What we come to realize is that, instead of aiming at the ultimate, once-and-for-all and definitely victorious battle of calmness/courtesy/distance-keeping against violence, we need to brace ourselves for an infinitely long string of 'proactive' counteractions. We seem to be settling for a prospect of a continuous and never conclusive war-to-exhaustion between 'good violence' (conducted in the service of law and order, however defined) and 'bad violence' (perpetrated for the purpose of undermining, breaking and incapacitating the current rendition of law and order) – 'bad' also for its insidious temptation to compel the forces of 'good violence' to adopt the tools and strategy of its enemy. We have to file a violence-free world among perhaps the most beautiful – though also, alas, the most out-of-reach – utopias.

How are we to account for that poorly anticipated (though no less radical and consequential for that reason) turn in the way we tend to think of the phenomenon of violence? That turn could have happened because of the sudden eruption of acts of violence being brought home by the ubiquitous and indefatigable media, after the pattern suggested by William Randolph Hearst's recipe for attention-grabbing news ('news ought to be served like coffee – fresh and hot'), in a way that literally forces them into our attention. And could that outburst of highly visible, palpable violence be seen as an effect of borders, (once imagined to be like impassable ramparts) having been made highly porous and osmotic – buffeted as they are by the swelling tides stirred and beefed up by the on-going processes of globalization?

Perhaps the shift in thought can be made intelligible as a derivative of the shift in practice by the states abandoning in deed, if not in so many words, their past ambition for a monopoly on the means and application of coercion? Or perhaps the right to draw the line between legitimate (i.e., serving the preservation of order) and illegitimate (i.e., disturbing or undermining that order) coercion, believed to be a prerogative of highly selective and definitely, unambiguously fixed agents, has joined the unstoppably lengthening roster of 'essentially contested' (to deploy Alfred North Whitehead's term) issues – and is now believed to be bound to stay forever contested. To take a leaf from the conceptual framework suggested by Snyder: contemporary states are currently plotted somewhere on the axis drawn between Max Weber's ideal type of the state holding a monopoly on the means of coercion and Snyder's 'failed' (or fallen, or felled) state – or, which amounts in practice to the same, a 'stateless territory'.

*

The right to draw (and redraw at will, if needed) the line between legitimate and illegitimate, permitted and prohibited, legal and criminal, tolerated and intolerable coercion is the principal stake in power struggles. Possession of such a right is, after all, the defining attribute of power – while the capability of using that right and rendering its use binding for others is the defining trait of domination. Establishing and executing that right was viewed since *Leviathan* as the domain of politics – a prerogative of, and a task to be accomplished by, the *government* standing for the *political* body. Closer to our time, that view has been extensively argued and emphatically reconfirmed by Max Weber (in his decision to define the political state by its monopoly on the means – and so, presumably, on the use – of coercion), acquiring an all but canonical status in social-political scholarship. Though, as Leo Strauss[2] warned insightfully on the threshold of our liquid-modern era, when discussing the precepts of the historicist approach to the human condition:

> there always have been and there always will be surprising, wholly unexpected, changes of outlook which radically modify the meaning of all previously acquired knowledge. No view of the whole, and in particular no view of the whole of human life, can claim to be final and universally valid. Every doctrine, however seemingly final, will be superseded sooner or later by another doctrine. (p. 21)

> All human thought depends on fate, on something that thought cannot master and whose workings it cannot anticipate. (p. 27)

> It is due to fate that the essential dependence of thought on fate is realized now, and was not realized in earlier times. (p. 28)

Back to Hobbes?

Two earlier-voiced, authoritative and seminal visions/ warnings jump to mind as laying the ground for Strauss' reasoning: Hegel's (of the Owl of Minerva that spreads its wings only with the falling of the dusk), and Marx's (of humans making history, albeit under conditions not of their choice). Between themselves, those three warnings/recommendations justify a thorough revision of Hobbes' vision of the state as the guarantor of its wards' security – and as its subjects' sole chance of defence against human intrinsic (instinctual and impulsive) aggressiveness, and so of being effectively protected from the unmanageable violence of others. They even suggest – even if obliquely – the possibility of listing the state, once described as the prime (or even the only) warrant of human security and the sole insurance against violence, among the prime factors/ causes/operators of the currently prevailing ambiance of un-safety and vulnerability to violence.

One of today's foremost, sharpest and most outspoken cultural/social critics, Henry Giroux – the author of *America's Addiction to Terrorism*, published by the *Monthly Review* – goes as far as concluding that:

> built into the system is a kind of systemic violence that's destroying the planet, all sense of public good and democracy – and it controls itself no longer by ideology, but by the rise of a punishing state – where everything is increasingly criminalized because it offers a threat to the financial elite and the control they have over the country ... Neoliberalism injects violence into our lives, and fear into our politics.[3]

I would add: and vice versa; violence into politics, and fear into our lives. And, saying 'ours', I wish to emphasize the impossibility of isolation from other people's gruesome fate in a world criss-crossed by information highways. People residing among the debris of the fallen states in the devilish belt between the tropics of Cancer and Capricorn, people with bodies and souls clotted with injections of fears and violence, come to *our* homes to roost – their all-too-visible, obtrusive, nagging and hugely discomforting presence in ever closer proximity to our homes as the impossible to overlook signals that, time and again, and with fast-rising frequency, challenge and defy our defensive inclination to stifle / suspend / repress into the subconscious the horrifying suspicion of the commonality, and growing similarity, of our respective fates. My mentioning lives injected with fear and violence refers therefore also to those among us who, day in, day out, cherish and enjoy the comforts of niches of 'law and order' – though, in moments of clarity, without being able to prevent suspicions and premonitions returning from their exile to the depths of the subconscious.

In the nutshell: courtesy of a long line of unanticipated turns of fate, the Leviathan came to be viewed as insolvent: unable to pay interest on the credit of trust that the seekers of security, on Hobbes' advice, used to invest in its assumed (sometimes feeling genuine, but ever too often putative) powers. On more and more occasions, it shows itself incapable of rendering the line it draws between legitimate and illegitimate violence truly reliable – obligatory, binding, unencroachable and impassable.

Max M. Mutschler of the BICC (Bonn International Centre for Conversion [from military to civilian purposes]) suggested in his March 2016 working paper that

Back to Hobbes?

Western states increasingly shy away from the use of own ground forces in their military interventions. Instead, they rely on precision strikes that are enabled by a network of sophisticated military technologies, including modern ground attack aircraft, unmanned aerial vehicles (UAVs), precision-guided munitions, air- and space-based sensors; all interlinked by modern communication technologies'.[4]

Mutschler traces these seminal departures in warfare back to the on-going process of de-territorialization of power, still gathering in force: 'Moving freely and, if necessary, out of reach of others to abdicate from one's responsibility, is the central feature of power in our time.'

In what I call liquid warfare, modern states shy away from the burdens and responsibilities of controlling and administrating territory because they believe that they have more cost-effective means of control at their disposal. Modern military technology enables them to decide when and where to attack, to strike the enemy with high precision while being inaccessible to any meaningful counterstrike. They rely on hit-and-run tactics, somewhat similar to central principles of guerrilla warfare, where mobility and speed trump sheer mass.

The emancipation of power from territory is the heaviest of blows that the far-from-finished process of globalization has delivered thus far to the standing function, and most seminally to the assumed omnipotence (and so the viability), of the Leviathan as described by Hobbes. Hobbes' Leviathan, whose model the modern states aimed and struggled to emulate, was visualized as a heavy and unwieldy, inert body, fixed firmly to the ground; in its essence, Hobbes' Leviathan was an 'anti-mobility' contraption: it was to be installed in order to render 'hitting and running' inconceivable. A Leviathan with porous, easily permeable territorial boundaries could not but be a jarring contradiction in terms. Such a porosity and permeability of frontiers has become, however, not just a local and contingent aberration, but well-nigh the norm of the new world (dis)order gestated in the course of progressive globalization of power coupled with continuing locality of politics; it was made viable, as well as sustained and reproduced, by the 'liquidization' of warfare and the technology that serves it. Politics – still the Leviathan-style modern state's principal, as much as monopolistic, *métier* – has knocked out its teeth that were meant to allow grasping and gnashing at the notoriously obstreperous and refractory powers, while the dentures intended to replace them showed themselves to be eminently frail and easily breakable.

In the result, the Leviathan has lost – in any but a purely formal sense – its assumed, and indeed commonly granted, monopoly on drawing the line separating the legitimate from illegitimate violence. The lines it still continues, by inertia, to mark, and attempts (or pretends to attempt) to fortify, are invariably contested in both theory and practice. Worse still: having put the task of repossessing its lost monopoly at the centre of its concerns and at the top of its *raisons d'être*, it found itself pushed/forced/obliged (but also willing) to subordinate all the rest of its extant duties to that purpose – if not to abandon them altogether – either through the ploy of washing its hands of its previously bequeathed and keenly adopted responsibility for the performance and its results, or through a subterfuge of 'outsourcing' them by contracting out or subsidiarizing to forces granted autonomy from its own interference. In consequence of all these departures, the state, for all practical intents and purposes, has replaced the role of a defender and guardian of security with that of one (though perhaps the most effective) among the manifold agents cooperating in raising insecurity, uncertainty and un-safety to the rank of permanent human conditions.

Those agents are indeed manifold and varied – though most of them (and arguably all) sprout from the same root: from the thorough globalization of human condition now slipping out of control and easily nipping in the bud or simply ignoring any inchoate attempt at supervision when confronted by the territorial and nominally sovereign state, shaped up historically (as Benjamin Barber reminds us) to promote autonomy, autarky and *independence* from extraterritorial powers and to perform the (now viewed as all but unfeasible) task of assuring security inside its territorial borders. While proceeding under conditions of uncontrollable – and in all probability irreversible – planet-wide *interdependence*, the inconceivability of the state acquitting itself of all such missions is a foregone conclusion.

I'll try to name and briefly describe just some of these agents – starting with the saturation of the planet with widely available, easy to obtain and easy to hide lethal weapons.

*

In 2003, 'Control Arms', a campaign jointly run by Amnesty International, International Action Network on Small Arms (IANSA) and Oxfam, so summarized the then situation in the global arms trade:[5]

The lack of arms controls allows some to profit from the misery of others. While international attention is focused on the need to control weapons of mass destruction, the trade in conventional weapons continues to operate in a legal and moral vacuum. More and more countries are starting to produce small arms, many with little ability or will to regulate their use. Permanent UN Security Council members – the USA, UK, France, Russia, and China – dominate the world trade in arms. Most national arms controls are riddled with loopholes or barely enforced. Key weaknesses are lax controls on the brokering, licensed production, and 'end use' of arms. Arms get into the wrong hands through weak controls on firearm ownership, weapons management, and misuse by authorized users of weapons.

Ten years and a major economic collapse later, on 2 March 2013, the *Guardian* reported: 'Despite the economic downturn it has been business as usual for the world's biggest arms companies who have seen sales of weapons and military services rise during 2010 and exceed $400bn (£250bn).'[6] And, after two years more, by August 2015, Amnesty International reported there were estimated to be 875 million small arms and light weapons in circulation worldwide, and between 700,000 and 900,000 small arms produced annually.[7]

Let me recall the advice that the great playwright Anton Chekhov, rightly adored and praised for the superb realism of his oeuvres, gave aspiring playwrights trying hard to follow his enticing achievement in reaching the heights of realism which were his trademark and to which he owed his world-wide fame – and eager to learn how to make their dream come true: if there is a rifle hanging on the wall in the first act of a play, it is bound to be discharged in the third.

It'd be utterly naive to expect that many, let alone most, of the close to 1 million annually produced small arms won't be discharged annually. We live in a world in which pragmatism is the topmost rationality: a world of 'I can, and *therefore* I shall and will.' A world in which Max Weber's idea of 'instrumental rationality' has been turned upside down: rather than in purposes seeking the most effective means, it now consists in the means that seek (and more often than not find) suitable applications. Such pragmatism is only to be expected, and has already – arguably – become un-detachable from our world of consumers: a world in which products, instead of answering to an already existing demand, are obliged and expected to create one and build it up – indeed, conjure it up, all too often *ab nihilo*.

When trying to visualize this aspect of our shared present-day condition, I find most adequate and useful the metaphor of a minefield, designed and deployed (though in a somewhat different context) by Yuri Lotman, the formidable Estonian student of culture on both its anthropological and historical planes. What we know of minefields for sure is that they are stuffed with explosives; what we reasonably guess is that sooner or later explosions must occur; but we have no inkling when and where they will happen next. The sole cure for this dreadful condition of awareness of the blows' imminence, combined with an incapacity to predict the place and time of their striking, is to abstain from mining the fields – a sound idea in itself, but, alas, a pipe-dream in our present condition.

A pipe-dream indeed, considering that the

military-industrial complexes of this world, particularly
in their present state of advanced emancipation from
political control, won't desist from their fabulous profits, while the governments of this world won't resist
the temptation to salvage employment statistics from
falling further that is offered by the thriving weapons
industry; and the criminals of the world won't miss
a chance of profiting from those (not many) governments that dare to brave the elements and, against all
odds, put constraints on exporting or importing guns or
explosives. Remember as well another temptation – one
that the holders of 'small arms', and particularly their
unscrupulous gurus and/or order-givers, find excruci-
atingly difficult to reject: a temptation offered by the
planetary media to inflate the impact and repercussions
of even the pettiest of small-town's discharges, to render
them visible and audible globally and in 'real time', and
to recycle them at no extra costs into globally blood-
curdling shocking events – casting life all around the
globe, in every nook and cranny of the planet, in a state
of permanent risk and emergency. And to top up the list
of factors making the disarming of minefields a pipe-
dream: the summary effect of all the already-mentioned
facts-of-the-matter is the growing conviction of the elec-
torates all over the world (with the US incontestably at
the top of the league) that more weapons, and making
them easier to obtain, are the best medicines against the
damage done by the saturation of the globe with weapons that are easy to obtain and easy to use.

*

Then there is the 'copycat' phenomenon – again greatly
facilitated by the ratings-greedy, and therefore ready-to-

oblige, media. Imitation follows the pattern of fashion; it derives, as do fashions, its overwhelming attraction from the promise to reconcile the irreconcilable and thereby to gratify simultaneously two human, all-too-human, cravings apparently at cross-purposes: the passion for sociality and the passion for individuality; the desire to belong and the desire to stand out. This kind of duality of intentions and the resulting dialectics of its behavioural impact have been spotted and extensively analysed by Georg Simmel.[8] Bringing to light the ostensibly timeless phenomenon of the dialectics of repetition and innovation inherent to fashion can, however, be traced back to Gabriel Tarde,[9] who explained the first by human actors' search for safe bets, triggered whenever they are faced with a risky choice; and the second by the similarly powerful yearning of the self for distinctiveness and autonomy.

Since the times of Tarde and Simmel, much has changed, however, in the mechanism, reach and role of *imitation* – and the new concept of the 'copycat' aims at grasping these recent alterations to the otherwise constant companion of the human mode of existence. The novelties in question have their roots in the quite recent revolution in communication, as analysed at length by Elihu Katz et al. in *Echoes of Gabriel Tarde: What We Know Better or Different 100 Years Later*.[10] To be sure, they are not entirely novelties; they are quantitative rather than qualitative changes to the circular movement between the source of information and individual opinions, together with conduct that follows – though the sheer massiveness and gravity of the quantitative changes prompted by the arrival of the Internet deserve to be acknowledged and admitted to amount to a new quality. They are fully and truly 'differences that make differences' (echoing the oft-stated adage 'difference that makes no differences is no difference').[11] All the same, credit needs to be given retrospectively to Tarde for signalling (well before its maturation, and before its presence had been noted and became impossible to overlook once it had been authoritatively endorsed by acknowledgment from the social sciences) the emergence of a pattern capable of producing, a century later, the present-day qualitative departure. As Elihu Katz points out in the Introduction to the quoted study above: 'Tarde realized that the crowd was being superseded by a new social formation that organized itself, virtually, around the daily newspaper. Rather than a physical assembly, the "public" was, in effect, a dispersed crowd that imbibed the daily agenda of the press and then reassembled, physically, in cafes, coffeehouses and salons to discuss current affairs, and form public opinion.'

With the benefit of hindsight, we can now, however, opine that the decisive, seminal and fateful step, already pregnant with the potential to gestate only in our time, was the separation of 'collective opinion' from the physical proximity of its carriers and promoters. At no stage of the opinion-formation process are a dense crowd and the physical density of face-to-face encounters nowadays (at any rate, in principle) necessary. Recognition of the profundity and enormous effects of the transformation of the public arena that this change augured and made possible, as well as highly likely to occur, needed many quantitative alterations, often too small to be instantly noted and recorded, for it to become clearly visible and be appreciated as such; for many decades, Tarde's ideas did not venture far outside the dusty covers of volumes hidden in the least frequently visited sections of academic libraries – while remaining conspicuous in academic debates solely by their absence. This, perhaps, was what Bruno Latour, as quoted by Katz, had in mind, when observing that Tarde 'needed a rather different century to be finally understood'.

We are now in that 'different century'. The motives guiding the dialectics of individual vs. group relationships (a sort of hate-love between the drive for the safety of belonging and the magnetic power of autonomous self-formation), intermittently bonding and courting divorce, might have emerged from that passage to a different century intact – but, as John B. Thompson[12] pointed out already twenty years ago, 'the development of communication media creates *new* forms of action and interaction and new kinds of social relationships [which] display a range of characteristics that differentiate them from face-to-face interaction' (pp. 81–2).

The meta-peculiarity of the new forms of communicative interaction and the new kind of social relationships they sediment – the matrix of all the rest of their peculiarities – is the growing prevalence of 'action at a distance'. Their consequence is the emergence of what Thompson calls 'mediated publicness': a kind of 'publicness' of 'individuals, actions and events' that is 'no longer linked to the sharing of a common locale' (p. 126). Thompson proposes to divide the forms of that relatively novel kind of action into two categories: one of 'mediated interaction', marked by the 'narrowing of symbolic cues' – as, for instance, 'winks, gestures, frowns and smiles' – 'which are available to the participants', and another of 'mediated quasi-interaction', adding yet

another peculiarity – of transmitting information produced 'for an indefinite range of potential recipients'
(pp. 83–4). I believe that the single most important feature (and a trait most relevant to the expansion of the
copycat phenomenon) of the new communication media
– and particularly of the Internet becoming accessible,
through a plethora of interactive and eminently *portable*
receivers, that, because of their small size, are available
for the 24/7 use for communication 'in real time' – is
that they make feasible the practising of a 'concerted
but uncoordinated responsive action' (p. 113). We may
say that what it makes possible (and well-nigh effortless – a quality that renders that possibility also highly
tempting) is the production in one go of myriads of
the proverbial 'messages in bottles', thereby multiply-
ing those messages' chances of being spotted, fished up,
opened, read and followed up, and making such concerted, though uncoordinated, conduct highly probable
– indeed, a common occurrence.

Published as it was twenty years ago, no wonder
Thompson's study focuses his analysis of the new communication media on the case of television – with its
sharp division and non-symmetry between producers
and recipients of information (coming close, one may
say – in its intention even more than in its practice – to
putting into operation Descartes' distinction between the
active, designing subject and the passive, pliable object).
I guess Thompson would have shifted that focus somewhat were his study conducted after the appearance of
the foremost novelty brought about by the Internet for
the practice of 'action at a distance': its in-built *inter-
activity*, which to a large (and perhaps growing) extent
blunts the Descartes-style sharpness of the subject/object

juxtaposition – a novelty whose profound consequences for the shape of human togetherness become, day in, day out, less doubtful as they grow more and more evident. When considering the prospects of 'publicness' – in other words, of a universally accessible public space, where everybody's ideas can (at least in principle) be put on display, got acquainted with, debated, approved or condemned – Thompson describes the 'symbolic environment' of that time as 'already shaped by substantial *concentrations* of resources' (p. 236, italics added) as the result of 'mergers, takeovers and cross-ownership in the media industries' (p. 241).

The correctness and veracity of that observation remain as sound today as they were twenty years ago. The advent of the Internet added, however, a new trend to the processes that marked the symbolic environment dominated by television: the process of the *dissipation* of resources which, despite the on-going rise in the power of media conglomerates, assists in establishing the regime of 'regulated pluralism' which Thompson offers as the principle fit to guide 'the reinvention of publicness' (p. 240). Pluralism is already here; and it is, indeed, increasingly *regulated*. With one or two crucial provisos, however: the task of regulating, like so many other aspects of human being-in-the-world (as, for instance, in the cases of concocting individual solutions to socially created problems, or composing a God 'of my own' from the offers made by organized religions) that 'regulation' has been 'subsidiarized' and left at the discretion of the individual. It has been relegated to Anthony Giddens' realm of 'life politics', but – courtesy of the Internet – life politics not only acquired access to, but subdued and conquered, the public arena, winning a no-longer-questioned, widely embraced rather than resented, as well as daily reproduced, domination. And another proviso: the emerging pluralism in question is – paradoxically – a derivative of the multitude of variegated individual attempts at 'regulating' (taming through reducing, or eliminating altogether) the confusing cacophony which such pluralism cannot but gestate and sustain – in other words, at making the indigestible palatable, and cutting the confusion down to the limits of intelligibility.

Cutting off its resident (more often than not a ship-wrecked resident, or one suspecting, and fretting about the likelihood of, a naval disaster) from the turbulent tides of the mind-bogglingly opaque pluralism, an island of tranquillity born of the marriage of transparency and un-ambiguity hits a bull's eye: it gratifies (or so it feels) simultaneously the yearning for belonging and the obligation of self-formation, inescapable and staunchly non-negotiable under liquid-modern conditions. Instead of being at loggerheads, the two demands intertwine and are (or at least appear to be) amenable to being answered concurrently, side by side, in one fell swoop. Copycat conduct is an ideal tool in attaining such an ideal solution to the double-pronged anxiety – and it is the Internet that enables the deployment of such a tool, virtually inapplicable in the endemically, irreducibly pluralist offline setting.

To have a chance of being copycatted, an act must first gain, however, the audience that the Internet provides; once wrapped, as they were in the by-now-distant past around neighbours in a physical proximity that made them available for repeatable face-to-face encounters, the groups of the informatics era (reincarnated in the shape of 'networks') are forming and gelling around those transmitters of information that, for one reason or another, are considered authoritative and believed to be trustworthy. The frequency of their appearance on screen, and yet more the numbers of 'likes' and 'sharings' they boast and duly add to their messages, provide (in the absence of more reliable, if less manipulable, measures) all the endorsement needed to show that their choice is publicly weighty and respected and so – by deduction – desirable. The fact that I've chosen them while rejecting or elbowing out the others on offer (unlike in the case of the community of yore, which used to choose *me* instead of being chosen *by me*, and to which I belonged without having been asked consent), feels blissfully and reassuringly like a pat on the shoulder of my self-esteem. It feels like an exercise in independence rather than dependency, and, in addition, like a gallant feat of self-assertion, with an added benefit of having been guaranteed recognition and group approval in advance.

*

These are features of all and any specimens of copycatting – but what we are interested in here is a special category of copycat conduct, of direct relevance to the issue of the noted growth in the volume and intensity of violence, oft perceived as a symptom of the return of the Hobbesian world (or, more correctly, the other way round: *our* return to Hobbes' world). What I have in mind is the rising frequency of copycat acts of violence.

Fitting rather well Jacques Derrida's model of 'iterations', those copycat acts are not carbon copies of the acts they copycat (given the cut-throat competition between media industries for ratings to be as high as possible and above all continuously rising – and so their consistent effort to serve the news, like coffee, fresh and hot in order to avoid the bane of their viewers' 'watching fatigue' – a mechanical, literally faithful, point-by-point reiteration would surely be counter-productive in the effort to get a share of the media-offered free publicity). Indeed, the copycat acts tend to be at the same time repetitious (aiming at borrowing some of the already-tested effects from the already-tested form of action) *and* innovative – adding one or a few spectacular touches previously unheard of, and so – hopefully – outdoing and overshadowing the shocks caused by the copycatted villainy. The second requirement – of something new and therefore carrying a fresh, not-yet-eroded supply of the shocking potential thanks to its unfamiliarity – is a necessary condition of the success of replicating the old.

For the copycatting of violent acts, offers sufficiently profuse to set at least a medium-term public agenda (with the dedicated and resourceful assistance of the media industry) are necessary; the aforementioned saturation of the globe with easy-to-obtain small weapons goes a rather long way to explaining their presence. But another condition must be met as well: a large enough demand for offers of this type. What is needed is a kind of demand that is already engaged in the search for effective, though convenient-to-use, tools for its gratification – while also being able, as well as likely, to find the act that is to be copycatted fit to gratify some already-formed and entrenched demands and expectations. The soil must be well primed for seeds to sprout.

*

Soil fertile for the sprouting of seeds of violence is nowadays in ample supply. It would be futile – indeed, inane – to charge the newly available informatics technology with responsibility for the appearance and spectacular proliferation of the copycat phenomenon; at the utmost, it may play an auxiliary, facilitating role in rendering the previously cumbersome and costly undertakings temptingly easy and seductively cheap. The seeds of violence would, however, have been found sterile and fruitless, if the soil on which they've been (however profusely) sprinkled were barren.

Well, barren it is not; quite the opposite – thanks to the plethora of fertilizers that the human condition is all too ready and keen to supply. Those fertilizers are many and varied, but one ingredient which each one of them needs to contain is anger – all the more rankling, festering and blistering because it is irritatingly and frustratingly short of an obvious, tested outlet. That anger torments wide and incessantly widening sectors of the population, though affecting them unevenly – for two starkly different reasons. Jock Young, an indefatigable and uniquely perceptive explorer of its roots, which are sunk deep in the vertigo of liquid-modern life, spells them out:

> The obsessive violence of the macho street gang and the punitive obsession of the respectable citizen are similar not only in their nature but in their origin. Both stem from dislocations in the labour market: the one from a market which excludes participation as a worker but encourages voraciousness as a consumer, the other from a market which includes, but only in a precarious fashion. That is, from tantalizing exclusion and precarious inclusion.[13]

As to the psychological mechanism of recycling the accumulated frustration and wrath into outbursts of violence, Young suggests: 'the transgressors are driven by the energies of humiliation – the utilitarian core is often there, but around it is constructed a frequent delight in excess, a glee in breaking the rules, a reassertion of manhood and identity'.[14]

What the above characteristics imply is that the acts of aggression are to a great extent disinterested (as in the popular formula 'nothing personal, Sir/Madam'), and lacking in what in detective dramas are called 'motives'. Their main – and arguably the only efficient – cause is all too often an overwhelming, uncontrollable build-up of anger, while the object of aggression is contingent, and only loosely – if at all (and unnecessarily) – related to its cause. The aggressiveness gestated by the unbearable sense of humiliation and abasement, or by the similarly unendurable horror of social degradation and exclusion, tends to be, as a rule, unfocused. Whether premeditated, deliberately chosen or accidental, the victim of a violent act tends to be an adventitious and random, as well as unplanned, side-effect of the un-knowability or un-reachability of a concrete target genuinely responsible for the aggressor's misfortune and anguish (even if a material link between the act and its object happens to be, more often than not, retrospectively implied).

In the case of acts of terrorism, their unfocused character and the randomness of their victims tend to be demonstrated and emphasized deliberately and explicitly, in a way impossible to overlook – with the intention to maximally expand the shocking impact of the terrorist act produced by a locally conceived and locally performed violence: the message conveyed by that randomness is that no one is safe; whether guilty or innocent, anybody – anytime and everywhere – could fall victim to future vengeful explosions of anger. Trying to prove to oneself and to others one's own non-involvement in causing the avenged injustice will be to no avail, and neither here nor there. The message intended to be sent by the calculated randomness of the outrage is that all of us, with no exception, have similarly valid reasons to be afraid of the prospect of experiencing first-hand, and personally tasting, the horrors of the victims' fate.

Letting out the accumulated anger is disinterested in the sense of being autotelic – its own motive and purpose; such an act is, as Willem Schinkel explained, a 'violence for the sake of violence'.[15] Schinkel suggests that 'autotelic aspects are present in every act of violence; violence is often selected not for the end it will secure, but for the intrinsic attractiveness of the act itself'. The morbid attraction of violence consists in bringing a temporary relief from the humiliating feeling of one's own inferiority – weakness, haplessness, indolence, nonentity: the kind of relief intimated millennia ago by Aesop in his allegory of the mollification and contentment felt by a perpetually frightened hare, always on the run from bigger and stronger animals, the moment it noticed a frog panicking in its turn and running for shelter at the first sign of this downcast and permanently despondent creature approaching.

Autotelic violence may serve as a sort of 'safety valve' that allows already-accumulated steam to be let off, yet it does little, if anything at all, to prevent the steam from accumulating again, reaching explosive density and a critical level of pressure. Getting an advantage over someone even weaker and less resourceful than myself comes easily – which is, simultaneously, its merit and demerit: its very facility robs it of the capacity of bringing the yearned-for satisfaction of 'a job well done'; it stops satisfaction well short of testifying to the attacker's superior skills and powers, and so also of assuring restoration of his self-esteem, self-respect and self-confidence. In this sense, the autotelic violence is also a meaningless violence; worst of all, it tends to be meaningless, painfully and dishonourably, to its perpetrator himself. What it loses in quality, it tries to compensate for by quantity. Meaningless violence tends to be self-propagating and self-amplifying.

Using one's own supreme might to maul and hurt an obviously weaker creature is a sort of menial, poor man's substitute for a 'real test' of capability, gallantry and courage, and, above all, of the mauler's own stature and significance. For the act of violence to become such a test, or at least amenable to being so presented, its perpetrator needs a *powerful* adversary to be challenged, injured and defeated: the more powerful, the better. Fighting Islamic malevolence and turning back the Muslim invasion that threatens to destroy 'everything we cherish and stand for' is an incomparably more effective cure for the self-derogation brought about by humiliation than setting fire to the stall of a Pakistani neighbour.

*

A certain Simone Simonini, the thoroughly negative hero (and the only imagined figure in a story in which all other actors are real historical personalities) of *The Prague Cemetery*[16] (the latest in the long line of Umberto Eco's novels to be distinguished by being remarkably well informed about the volatile spirit and convoluted meanders of European history), offers a uniquely profound insight into the genealogy of the paranoid spectre of conspiracy, always close to the threshold of awareness even when it's napping, but now wide awake. This is how Eco, through the lips of Simonini, summarizes the service provided by the conspiracy worldview, its utility and the causes of its extensive appeal:

I have known many people who feared the conspiracy of some hidden enemy – for my grandfather it was the Jews, for the Jesuits it was the Masons, for my Garibaldian father it was the Jesuits, for the kings of half Europe it was the Carbonari, for my Mazzinian companions it was the king backed by the clergy, for the police throughout the world it was the Bavarian Illuminati, and so forth. Who knows how many other people in this world still think they are being threatened by some conspiracy. Here's a form to be filled out at will, by each person with their own conspiracy. (p. 99)

In his lecture given at the University of Bologna at the inauguration of the 1994/5 academic year, and published in the collections of essays[17] analysing the respective roles of truth and falsity in history (the false, he says, 'not necessarily in the form of lies but surely in the form of error', has motivated 'many events in history' (p. 2), though sometimes for better, some other times for worse) – based on exquisitely erudite explorations of the widely influential stories of hidden (as a rule, malevolent) conspiracies and plots guiding from behind the scenes the course of history, and so also the fate of their 'auctors' (that is, its authors in cahoots with its actors) – Umberto Eco points out: 'The myth of the secret societies and the existence of Superior Unknowns who directed the fate of the world already were debated before the French Revolution.' Those mythical stories were on the whole 'too fascinating to be derailed by fact' (pp. 18–19): 'Each of these stories had a virtue: as narratives, they seemed possible, more than everyday or historical reality, which is far more complex and less credible. The stories seemed to explain something that was otherwise hard to understand' (p. 23).

The narrator of *The Prague Cemetery* lives, thinks and acts in the nineteenth century, but Umberto Eco, who put him there, recomposed his life, thought and actions with the twenty-first century's benefit of hindsight. Far from being a mental aberration of a tiny deranged margin, the conspiracy theory of history and of the alleged/putative machinery pulling in our time the strings of the world's actors, is moving steadily closer to the heart of political debate and the public opinion it feeds and inspires; in a growing number of countries (even those that have until recently been believed to be effectively immune to its bacilli), it tends to be ominously fast-rising in popularity, acquiring ever expanding constituency, ever more often cropping up in politicians' speeches and mass media broadcasts, as well as occupying a rapidly expanding sector of the so-called 'social website' exchanges. Its rise in stature is anything but easy to oppose, let alone to arrest, in as far as inscribing the acts of 'autotelic violence' into the wide – perhaps (who knows?) infinitely wide – canvas of a 'world-wide conspiracy' raises their significance immensely, as well as upgrading their executioners' scores of gallantry and importance.

The added – and perhaps the paramount – asset of

such inscription consists in casting the nets even wider
than before: catching recruits from the milieus resistant
to, or even opposing, copycat cases of autotelic violence, while craving a 'big cause' able to inject meaning
(a noble, of course, as well as ennobling meaning) into
their otherwise bleak and insipid, prospectless existence.
Having a cause means reaching far beyond the locality
of the event: rising tides bound to inundate immeasur-
ably more extensive spaces and affecting uncountable
masses of people; a cause coming close to the pattern
set by the War of the Worlds or the last, final contest
between Good and Evil: a battle of giants, the life-and-
death combat, the war till exhaustion and so, indeed,
the last war – a war to finish all wars and a victory to
preclude any future defeat.

*

This brings us to the phenomenon of 'suicide terrorism'
– itself a case of a copycatting of sorts: a distant, updated
– indeed, a 'new and improved' ('improved', if measured
by the level of its spectacularity and the scope and duration of its psychological reverberations) – version of the
Japanese 'kamikaze' of the time of the Second World
War. This time over, the growing numbers of people –
mostly young men and women – willing to sacrifice their
life for a 'cause' is, however, not so much the outcome
of ideological fanaticism and totalitarian pressures as
the consequence of harsh living conditions and fading
life prospects. Their readiness for sacrifice tends to be
aided and abetted by the policies of exclusion adopted
by powers-that-be as their principal strategy of social
domination in general, and as the favourite technique of
governance in particular – as well as by the progressive

outsourcing of the regulatory tasks and credentials of the elected state organs to the vagaries of markets, and so to agents and factors well beyond the reach of the means available to the 'individual', now decreed to tackle life's challenges using her/his own (in most cases, grossly inadequate) resources. As Stanley Cohen points out in his trail-blazing study *Visions of Social Control*:

> The combination of welfare cut-backs and the illusory qualities attributed to 'community' has meant that the ill, the inadequate and the defective, receive little in the way of constructive social intervention. Shunted between public welfare roles and the private sector, they find themselves in communities unable to tolerate or look after them. For criminals and delinquents, there is indeed intervention, but the new agencies can hardly be said to be responding to the wider social contexts (class, race, power, inequality) in which crime and delinquency are located.[18]

There is widespread and well-grounded belief that the blame for today's growth of violence, particularly dense and intense in the underprivileged, poor and deprived urban areas, falls to a considerable extent on the dominant consumerist culture, in which most of the 'normal', *comme il faut, bona fide* members of the present-day society, as much as their violent attackers, are born, brought up and trained/seduced to keenly participate.[19] As I wrote, five years ago, on the aftermath of the Lewisham riots in London:

> From cradle to coffin we are trained and drilled to treat shops as pharmacies filled with drugs to cure or at least mitigate all illnesses and afflictions of our lives and lives in common. Shops and shopping acquire thereby a fully and

truly eschatological dimension. Supermarkets, as George Ritzer famously put it, are our temples; and so, I may add, the shopping lists are our breviaries, while strolls along the shopping malls become our pilgrimages. Buying on impulse and getting rid of possessions no longer sufficiently attractive in order to put more attractive ones in their place are our most enthusing emotions. The fullness of consumer enjoyment means fullness of life. I shop, therefore I am. To shop or not to shop, this is the question.

For defective consumers, those contemporary have-nots, non-shopping is the jarring and festering stigma of a life un-fulfilled – and of their own nonentity and good-for-nothingness. Not just the absence of pleasure: absence of human dignity. Of life meaning. Ultimately, of humanity and any other ground for self-respect and respect of the others around.[20]

'Unwertes Leben' ('life unworthy of living') was originally a label attached by tyrannical rulers to the categories of population they declared unfit and undesirable due to being a burden or a menace to a nation, class, race or religion. Increasingly, the matter of adopting or rejecting that label is, in our times, 'subsidiarized' to the individual abandoned to stew in his/her own juice: a question of individual choice rather than a from-on-high decree by authoritarian powers. A growing number of individuals prefer that choice to a kind of life lived under conditions that they not only find unendurable, but also suspect, for a valid reason, will remain so for its duration. The choice of a 'meaningful death' appears to them a better option (all too often, incomparably better) to a hopelessly meaningless life, its only realistic alternative. It is from among such individuals, or whole categories of such individuals, that the commanders of terrorist gangs recruit their obedient soldiers ready for self-sacrifice. The sole task left to the recruiters is to brainwash the recruits into believing in the meaningfulness of the form and time of dying they suggest – the task made all the easier to perform by the soldiers who, well before joining them, had already been convinced of the meaninglessness of life.

*

Hobbes' pre-Leviathan world, let us recall, the world knowing of no politics and no politically conceived and born powers, was a theatre of war: a war of *all* against *all*, and so a war conducted by, and against, no one in particular. *Every* man or woman was up in arms against *every* other man and woman. Every 'other' was either an already unmasked enemy, or an enemy yet to be unmasked. Antennae had to be stretched and tuned in all directions. Permanently. Safety was a bluff. A moment of tranquillity could be only the enemy's ploy, meant to lay vigilance to a nap. Were the Hobbesian pre-state creatures in possession of powder, they would've surely kept it dry – at all times and under any circumstance (except when putting it to its pre-designed and predestined use).

As we *feel* it to be (even if we can't put a name on that feeling), our world – the world of weakening human bonds, of deregulation and atomization of politically constructed structures, of divorce between politics and power – is again a theatre of war: a war of all against all, and so a war conducted by, and against, no one in particular. Conducted, day in, day out, either individually or (occasionally) in ad hoc or more durable alliances – day in, day out a-changing. By the united forces of markets, teachers in our schools, managers in our work-places, and the media portraying for our instruction and consumption the world we are predestined to inhabit, we are, from our early childhood, groomed and honed to spend our life serving as soldiers in that war – though now stripped of the state-issued uniforms and re-named as 'competing individuals'. As Frank Bruni of the *New York Times* found out, the admissions process for the leading educational establishments – the most prestigious, authoritative stage-setting colleges of this world – 'warps the values of students drawn into a competitive frenzy'.[21] We are all each other's competitors: either already unmasked as such, or certain to be unmasked at the first opportunity. People in a 'competitive frenzy' tend to keep their powder dry and barrels well lubricated – always close to hand and ready for use.

We are being taught self-reliance – which translates as being trained to be, at any moment, determined and ready – and to count on no one but ourselves when we happen to fall into trouble and need to escape from muddy and turbulent waters into clear and tranquil ones. The order of things may be not of our own making, but it is us, each one of us, that must, 24/7, play its guardian. The playing we lean over backward to do – but *to be*?! Sooner or later, almost all of us have to make the gruesome discovery that – as Anand Giridharadas, quoted by David Brooks in the same issue of the *New York Times*,[22] suggests – 'if anything unites America in this fractious moment it is a widespread sentiment that power is somewhere other than where you are'. Giridharadas dubs that all-but-universal sentiment 'an anxiety of impotence'.

As the Pew Research Center, also quoted by Brooks,

found out: in reply to the question 'Would you say your side has been winning or losing more?', 64 per cent of Americans chose the second option. I suspect that the percentage of those choosing that option would be higher yet – and perhaps considerably higher – were it not for the Americans and all the rest of us having been trained/drilled, as we are, in measuring our own value by the strength of our own feet, on which we are expected to stand; being taught to feel ashamed to admit just how unreliable our wobbly legs are to the strangers asking such a personal question – the self-esteem's version of 'to be or not to be'. The sentiment of impotence and the dread/jitters it gives rise to are highly embarrassing conditions which most of us would loathe to divulge, and be aghast to be caught in. Absolute power – as folk wisdom has insisted since at least Lord Acton – may be corrupting absolutely; but in order to update that wisdom to the conditions of our deregulated/atomized society, Brooks makes us aware that the feeling of absolute powerlessness can also corrupt absolutely:

> Today we live in a world of isolation and atomisation, where people distrust their own institutions. In such circumstances many people respond to powerlessness with pointless acts of self-destruction. In the Palestinian territories, for example, young people don't organize or work with their governments to improve their prospects. They wander into Israel, try to stab a soldier or a pregnant woman and get shot or arrested – every single time. They throw away their lives for a pointless and usually botched moment of terrorism.

However illusory such a moments of power might be, they are all too often hoped (hoped *against* hope) to be

capable of compensating for the all-too-palpably enduring powerlessness – and, obliquely, to repay and avenge
the both protracted and brutal denial of meaningful life.
One may deride the naivety of that hope, or feel baf-
fled by the enormity of the price some people are ready
to pay for putting that hope to an (a priori abortive
and doomed) test; and yet many others may well perceive that hope as the only realistic, attainable chance
of rehabilitation and repossession of their treacher-
ously, viciously stolen dignity. And the knife-carrying
Palestinians are but one case in the long list of people
exposed to multiple human-dignity-and-respect-denying
oppressions.

As to those on the other pole of the well-being scale,
the Americans, citizens of the richest and most powerful country on the planet, they (in David Brooks'
words): 'are beset by complex, intractable problems
that don't have a clear villain: technological change dis-
places workers; globalization and the rapid movement
of people destabilize communities; family structure dis-
solves; the political order in the Middle East teeters,
the Chinese economy craters, inequality rises, the global
order frays, etc.'.

One is tempted to say that, in comparison with
the Americans smarting under blows, yet unaware
where they fall from and by whom they are delivered,
Palestinians are lucky in being at least able to lay the
guilt for all their sufferings on the common denominator
of all hardships: the Israeli occupation. The others elsewhere, in a similar no-prospects no-dignity plight, have
little idea whom they should stab with the knives they
carry. They strike at random. Life in our updated version of the Hobbesian world is akin to walking through

a minefield whose maps were never sketched or have been lost – a field, let me remind you, so teeming with explosives that explosions cannot but occur time and again, but no one can say with any degree of certainty where and when.

And so it seems that we are entitled to remove the question mark following this chapter's title. We are indeed back in, or at any rate on the road leading back to, Hobbes' world – though this time we are finding ourselves in the condition of war of all against all not because of the *absence* of an almighty Leviathan, but because of the co-presence of numerous, all-too-numerous, big, small and tiny Leviathans, gravely malfunctioning and failing to perform the tasks for whose sake our ancestors, in Hobbes' opinion, invited (or, rather than that, conjured up) the Leviathan to rule them. And because *the* Leviathan – a Leviathan capable of curing the lesser Leviathans' flaws and deficiencies (defects among which the fact that our mode of togetherness lags far behind its novel, but already firmly entrenched, conditions, takes pride of place) is nowhere in sight.

2

Back to Tribes

'If states ever become large neighbourhoods, it is likely that neighbourhoods will become little states. Their members will organize to defend their local politics and culture against strangers. Historically, neighbourhoods have turned into closed and parochial communities . . . whenever the state was open' – so Michael Walzer retrospectively concluded over thirty years ago from the theretofore-accumulated experience of the past, presaging its repetition in the imminent future.[1] That future, having turned into the present, confirmed his expectation and thus reasserted his diagnosis.

Courtesy of globalization and of the ensuing separation and divorce of power and politics, states are indeed turning presently into not much more than larger neighbourhoods, confined to the inside of only vaguely delineated, porous and ineffectually fortified borders – whereas the neighbourhoods of yore, once anticipated to accompany the rest of *pouvoirs intermédiaires* on their journey into the dustbin of history, struggle to take on the role of 'little states', making the most of what has

---

been left of quasi-local politics and of the state's once jealously guarded unshared and inalienable monopolist prerogative of setting 'us' apart from 'them' (and, of course, vice versa).

Once the job of drawing borders, digging moats and building walls topped with barbed wire starts in earnest, all and any 'differences that people can point out . . . are used to justify superiority of one group over another. The gun lovers think they are superior to the gun haters because they love guns, and the gun haters think they are superior to the gun lovers because they hate guns'; 'Why are differences between population groups always reduced to an inferior/superior relationship? Tribalism is why'; 'And the purpose of the tribe is to determine whom to support and whom to kill.'[2]

The terms selected to perch the issue on a knife-edge and keep it there for the duration tend to be harsh and intransigent (reconciliation of differences, hybridization or gelling may occasionally happen there – but if they do, they are seldom if ever intended and even less frequently desired). When perched on a knife-edge, the uncompromisingly divisive/separating precept 'either–or' is as self-evident as it is obligatory, while the alternative maxim, 'and–and', is cast off limits, together with the well-nigh-inconceivable abstention from making the choice between two alternative tenets unambiguous and irrevocable. Under such circumstances, 'no one listens to anyone. Any information that contradicts what either party is arguing, is ignored . . . People don't listen to each other, because they really don't hear each other. Information that supports their beliefs is emotionally significant and is processed. Everything else is thrown away',[3] or – preferably – never allowed to get in.

In a territory populated by tribes, conflicting sides shun and doggedly desist from persuading, proselytizing, or converting each other; the inferiority of a member – any member – of an alien tribe is and must need be, and remain, a predestined – eternal and incurable – liability, or at least is seen and treated as such. The inferiority of the other tribe must be its ineffaceable and irreparable condition, and its indelible stigma beyond repair – bound to resist all and any attempt at rehabilitation. Once the division between 'us' and 'them' has been performed according to such rules, the purpose of any encounter between the antagonists is no longer its mitigation, but a gaining/creating of yet more proof that mitigation is contrary to reason and out of the question. To let the sleeping dog lie and avert misfortune, members of different tribes locked in a superiority/inferiority loop talk not to, but past, each other.

This is how Luc Boltanski describes the emergent hegemonic philosophy (as Antonio Gramsci could probably have classified the present 'back to tribes' trend), concentrating on its French variety, the 'new dominant ideology, or neo-conservatism French style':

> It is marked, simultaneously, by anti-capitalism (in distinction from the American neo-conservatism), moralism and xenophobia. In an almost obsessive fashion it focuses on the issue of national identity, on the opposition between the genuine (and good) French people and the immigrants in *banlieues*, amoral, violent and dangerous – and above all bent on profiting from the goodness of the welfare state [in French called, yet more poignantly, l'État-providence].[4]

And he adds: having condemned and dismissed the official policy of tolerance for amounting to laxity, the neo-conservative ideology 'demands reinforcement of police powers'.

*

Following Rozenblit's suggestion that 'Tribalism is why', we are, however, likely (as well as being recommended) to ask 'why tribalism?'

As Celia de Anca suggests,[5] the re-emergence of 'emotionality' from its lengthy twentieth-century exile (aided and abetted, in her view – or even exacerbated and beefed up – by the new managerial policy of corporations eager to 'tap into the forces resulting from the diversity among company employees') bears responsibility for the astounding progress of the new wave of tribalism: 'The main change of paradigm we are witnessing is *a shift from a longing for independence from a society made up of communities, to a longing for belonging to a society made up of individuals.*'

To put it in the nutshell: from the long modern war-to-exhaustion waged under the banner of rationality, efficiency and utility against choice-constraining social/moral bonds, obligations and commitments, it was the self-identifying and self-asserting individual who ultimately emerged victorious; the victory, however, was soon found to be only pyrrhic – as the 'negatively free' (in the terms of Isaiah Berlin's dichotomy) victor was abandoned to his or her own lamentably inadequate resources, emotionally desiccated, and all but 'positively impotent' (that is, freed from outside interference together with outside help – and so stripped of the social capital indispensable for acting effectively, and indeed for making really consequential use of the hard-won right to self-assertion). Such freedom bore little likeness to the blissful dreams and seductive promises accompanying the war for the individual's standing and the emancipation of subjectivity. Individual liberty paid for with individual security felt less and less as a good bargain – and more and more like falling from a pan into the fire.

De Anca is hopeful. She believes her 'change of paradigm' not to be a return to the past version of a society 'made up of communities' with all their hotly resented aspects, but a leap forward, towards removal – or at least a radical reduction – of the notorious friction between the 'individual capacity for independent thinking' and 'the need to belong to a group' – which 'do not need to be incompatible': a move not so much back to tribalism, as 'beyond tribalism' (or, rather, beyond the tribalism vs. anti-tribalism quandary), towards 'new forms of ethnicity' offering 'the sense of totally belonging to a community without losing individual consciousness'. She welcomes such innovations, which she believes to be already in place: in the 'new forms of tribalism' she spies the model of 'open-ended communities, with weaker emotional attachments than in previous tribal modes'. In spelling out her conviction, she relies mostly on the concepts born inside the 'political and economic organizations in the world today' and developed by their 'well-known consultants who work on many programs helping them': in short, she makes her wager on the emergent philosophy of management, possibly holding a chance of rising to near-universal dominance.

Bent on shifting the chores of management down the hierarchy of command – on 'subsidiarizing' the task of 'bringing results', together with the responsibility for

Retrotopia

failure, to their subordinates, the 'advanced managerial philosophy and policy' of the day finds, in the widespread yearning for the combination of the safety of belonging with unwillingness to renounce the benefits of individual autonomy, a welcome opportunity to expand profits and gains and cut down on expenditures. In the current version of managerial newspeak, the intentionally foggy and under-defined idea of 'open-ended community' serves primarily as a cover-up for the practice of disablement sold under the name of enablement. Personal idiosyncrasies – emotional attachments and allergies, sympathies and antipathies, preferences and repulsions, likes and dislikes – all those individual, non-serial qualities, motives and inclinations that once had to be left in the cloakroom at the entrance to the factory or office building, are not just allowed and tolerated inside those buildings, but keenly invited to enter and stay, as well as heartily commended and vigorously encouraged in all those aspiring to admission or already admitted; individual idiosyncrasies tend to be treated as integral parts of job-description and principal criteria deployed in the evaluation of the employee's performance. Variety is the declared and pursued goal, whereas homogeneity and repetitive routines are censured and shunned for being perceived as counterproductive and unprofitable.

Henry Ford's conveyer belts and assembly lines, as well as Frederick Taylor's time and motion measurements, are out – but instead the employees directed to become and stay, as well as to act like, individuals are charged with the intentionally vague task of dovetailing their individually undertaken and performed acts to the 'assembly line' of company profit-making. That seminal change in the status of traits previously ear-

54

marked for elimination from the workplace – or at the least for suppression during working hours – intends to cater, simultaneously, to the employees' ambitions of self-assertion and their nostalgia for the emotional warmth of belonging (now postulating, and promising, recognition and approval of individual choices). What, however, all such departures in our thoroughly deregulated labour market and labour condition deliver in practice is an obligation to contribute to the 'wellness' of the 'open-ended [?] community' with no attached guarantee of mutuality – let alone any insurance against failure to rise to the standards of expectations kept perpetually under-defined and left to the volatile discretion of the managerial version of 'community elders'.

To cut the long story short: the sought-after benefits of belonging vanish somewhere in the process of 'community building' thus defined. And to add insult to that injury, instead of buying a specific duration of labour and specific trade skills of labourers relevant to the specific job they have been hired to perform, the company can now plead its right to exploit the totality of time and the sum total of personality assets of the employee – or even tacitly expect its employees to be 24 hours a day, 7 days a week, on service, without that service having been explicitly demanded, let alone written into the contract.

Going 'beyond tribalism', by reconciling the irreconcilable – achieving and collating 'the best of both (that is, the community's and individuality's) worlds' – looks suspiciously like the managers' of the day, and their consultants', attempt to capitalize on the grassroots' 'back to tribes' sentiments and mindset, both gestated by factors rooted well outside the reach of the company managers' powers, rather than a utopia of a better society visualized and promised to be pursued by the new philosophers and practitioners of the managerial art.

*

In the *Eighteenth Brumaire of Louis Bonaparte*, Karl Marx explained the mystery of revolutions kicking wide open the door to the future – unknown, not yet existing, untried, never before lived through, and for those reasons unexplored and at best vaguely guessed – while dressed in made-to-order replicas of the original old clothes stored in museums or in attire copying that once donned (or believed to have been donned) by the heroes of the past on display in Madame Tussaud's waxworks museum or its numerous variants:

> Men make their own history, but they do not make it as they please; they do not make it under self-selected circumstances, but under circumstances existing already, given and transmitted from the past. The tradition of all dead generations weighs like a nightmare on the brains of the living. And just as they seem to be occupied with revolutionizing themselves and things, creating something that did not exist before, precisely in such epochs of revolutionary crisis they anxiously conjure up the spirits of the past to their service, borrowing from them names, battle slogans, and costumes in order to present this new scene in world history in time-honoured disguise and borrowed language.

Focusing his attention on the series of French nineteenth-century political upheavals, Marx unravels the psycho-social logic of turning to the past for support in opening to the future the gates of the present:

Lacking in heroism as bourgeois society is, it nevertheless stood in need of heroism, of self-sacrifice, of terror,
of civil war, and of bloody battle fields to bring it into
the world. Its gladiators found in the stern classic traditions of the Roman republic the ideals and the form, the
self-deceptions, that they needed in order to conceal from
themselves the narrow bourgeois substance of their own
struggles, and to keep their passion up to the height of a
great historic tragedy.[6]

Indeed, the resurrection of the tribal mentality briefly
characterized at the start of this chapter looks much like
a more or less spontaneous public response to the far-
reaching but incoherent transformations in existential
conditions that between themselves amount to making
the present look and feel a no less 'foreign country'
than (to follow David Lowenthal's memorable thirty-
year-old diagnosis and title) the past has been in our
fast-changing modern world, notoriously surprising and
known to be stubbornly, repeatedly baffling its residents
and catching them unprepared: taking them aback, dis-
orienting and confusing them. Being a foreign country
stopped being a particular and exclusive quality of the
past, and in the result the boundary separating the past
from the present has been progressively washed out and
border-posts all but vacated. The future, of course, is
also a foreign country – though one can note among our
contemporaries interest in fencing ourselves up from
the future more strictly and impermeably than from the
past: the numbers of tourists looking forward to visit-
ing and exploring the foreign country of the future is
falling fast, and by now is limited to the most opti-
mistic and adventurous (and, according to some, the

most light-hearted and happy-go-lucky) among us. The number of people hurrying to travel there in the hope of finding the future full of more pleasurable experiences than successive lived-through presents have been, seems to be falling even more quickly; our sci-fi films and novels are more and more often catalogued in the sections of horror movies and gothic literature.

These days we tend to fear the future, having lost trust in our collective ability to mitigate its excesses, to render it less frightful and repellent, as well as somewhat user-friendlier. What we still, by inertia, call 'progress' evokes nowadays emotions opposite from those that Kant, who coined the concept, meant it to arouse. More often than not, it evokes the fear of an impending catastrophe instead of the joy of more comfort approaching and more worrisome inconvenience being about to perish and be cast into oblivion.

The first thing to leap to mind whenever 'progress' is mentioned is, for many of us, the prospect of more jobs for humans – those requiring intellectual skills as much as the already-vanished manual ones – that are bound to soon disappear, replaced by computers and computer-managed robots; and of yet steeper hills up which the battle for survival will need to be fought. According to almost all available research, the 'millennials' – the young people currently entering the labour market, facing the challenges of adult self-reliance and the uncertainties endemic to the search for a decent, satisfactory, gratifying and recognized social position – are the first post-war generation to voice a fear of losing instead of raising, the social standing achieved by their parents; most 'millennials' expect their future to bring worsening of their life conditions, instead of paving the way to their further improvements that marked their parents' life story and which their parents taught them to expect and to work for. All in all, the vision of unstoppable 'progress' portends the menace of loss instead of auguring new attainments and moving up in the world; it is now associated more with social degradation than with advancement and promotion. Meanwhile, as David Lowenthal pointed out in his next study,[7] 'as hopes of progress fade, heritage consoles us with tradition'.

'Why does heritage loom so large today?', Lowenthal asks; and, seeking for the answers:

> Answers differ from place to place ... But no explanation specific to one people can account for a trend so contagious. What is involved is a cluster of trends whose premises, promises, and problems are truly global. These trends engender isolation and dislocation of self from family, family from neighbourhood, neighbourhood from nation, and even oneself from one's former selves. Such changes reflect manifold aspects of life – increasing longevity, family dissolution, the loss of familiar surroundings, quickened obsolescence, genocide and wholesale migration, and a growing fear of technology. They erode future expectations, heighten past awareness, and instil among millions the view that they need and are owed a heritage ... Beleaguered by loss and change, we keep our bearings only by clinging to the remnants of stability.[8]

Having found that much, he warns, repeatedly: 'Ignorance, like distance, protects heritage from harsh scrutiny.' But vagueness and ignorance have also another virtue: 'The past is more admirable as a realm of faith than of fact' (pp. 134–5).

In conclusion of his monumental, multi-faceted study,

Lowenthal suggests that 'myopic rivalry is . . . endemic to the very nature of heritage. To insist we were the first or the best, to celebrate what is ours and excludes others, is what heritage is all about' (p. 239).

> Heritage builds collective pride and purpose, but in so doing stresses distinctions between good guys (us) and bad guys (them). Heritage faith, heritage commodities, and heritage rhetoric inflame enmity, notably when our unique legacy seems at risk. Entrenched myopia foments strife; ignorance inhibits reciprocity. Besotted by our heritage, blind to that of others, we not only eschew comparison but forfeit its benefits. (pp. 248–9)

*

A neighbourhood filled by strangers is a visible, tangible sign of certainties evaporating, and the prospects of life – as well as the fate of pursuit of them – drifting out of control. Strangers stand for everything evasive, feeble, unstable and unforeseeable in life that poisons the daily bustle with premonitions of our own impotence and the sleepless nights filled with nightmarish forebodings. It is, first and foremost, against the strangers (and, in the first place, the 'blatantly outlandish' – aliens, foreigners, immigrants) – for the sake of getting rid of strangers – that the residents of an infested neighbourhood (to recall Michael Walzer) 'will organize to defend their local politics and culture' and would try to recast it into a 'little state'. Considering, however, that conjuring up a future state cleansed of strangers is hardly on the cards and, in all probability, is beyond the realm of the possible, the image picked to guide the effort of that recasting is all too often one drawn from the past (the past as it *was* – but even more often as it *could be* imagined: unambiguously 'ours', unspoiled by 'their' obtrusive proximity).

Once stripped of power to shape the future, politics tends to be transferred to the space of collective memory – a space immensely more amenable to manipulation and management, and for that reason promising a chance of blissful omnipotence long (and perhaps irretrievably) lost in the present and in the times yet to come. Most obviously – and therefore most damagingly to our self-confidence, self-esteem and self-pride – we are not the ones who control the present from which the future will germinate and sprout – and for that reason we entertain little, if any, hope of controlling that future; in the course of its formation we seem to be doomed to remain pawns on someone else's chessboard and in someone else's – yet someone unknown and unknowable – game. What a relief, therefore, to return from that mysterious, recondite, unfriendly, alienated and alienating world, densely sprinkled with traps and ambushes, to the familiar, cosy and homely, sometimes wobbly but consolingly unobstructed and passable, world of memory: *our* memory – and so *my*, as I'm one of '*us*', memory; *our* memory – memory of *our*, not their, past; a memory – to be possessed (that is, used and abused) by *us* and by us *alone*.

In *theory*, future is the realm of freedom (everything may yet happen there) – as distinct from the past, the realm of immutable and inalterable inevitability (everything that could've happened did); future is in principle pliable – the past is solid, sturdy and fixed once and for all. Whereas, in the *practice* of the politics of memory, future and past had their attitudes exchanged, or at least were treated as if they did. Pliability and manageability of the past, its susceptibility to moulding and remoulding, are simultaneously the *sine qua non* condition of the *politics* of memory, its well-nigh axiomatic presumption of legitimacy, and its acquiescence to perpetually re-enacted creation.

In contemporary society, the principal aim of the politics of historical memory is the justification of the entitlement of the group (called 'nation') to territorially delineated political sovereignty – which in turn is the principal aspiration and objective of nationalism. As Ernest Gellner memorably put it:

> Nationalism is primarily a political principle, which holds that the political and national unit should be congruent
> . . . Not only is our definition of nationalism parasitic on a prior and assumed definition of the state; it also seems to be the case that nationalism emerges only in milieus in which the existence of the [territorially sovereign] state is already taken for granted.[9]

As he added, the marriage of state and nation is a historical contingency, not a law of nature, though the functions of nationalism is to deny the first and affirm the second, and to entrench in the final result the idea that 'a man must have a nationality as he must have a nose and two ears; a deficiency in any of these particulars is not inconceivable and does from time to time occur but only as a result of some disaster, and it is itself a disaster of a kind' (p. 8).

One way or another, nationalism would be all but unthinkable, or at any rate a phenomenon exceedingly unlikely to emerge, were it not for the idea of the territorially sovereign state (*cuius regio, eius religio*, a formula originally designed at the 1648 Westphalian Conference conducted in Münster and Osnabrück, and then – beginning from the 'The Spring of Nations' of 1848, and forcefully confirmed by Woodrow Wilson during the 1919 Versailles Peace Conference – rearticulated for all practical intents and purposes as *cuius regio, eius natio*). Modern nationalism was and remains a power struggle, and the hotly desired stake of that power contest, and the exceedingly attractive and seductive spoils of insurrections and civil or international military and diplomatic conflicts, is and remains the possession of a politically independent, sovereign territorial state. To quote from Gellner once more: 'Nations as a natural, God-given way of classifying men, as an inherent though long delayed political destiny, are a myth; nationalism, which sometimes takes pre-existing cultures and turns them into nations, sometimes invents them, and often obliterates pre-existing cultures, *that* is a reality, for better or worse, and in general an inescapable one' (p. 47).

Inescapability chimes well with the avidly desired, while stubbornly missing, firm ground beneath the feet – buffeted as they currently are by cross-tides of mutually falsifying and cancelling messages. In 'The Multiplication of the Media', one of the essays included in *Faith in Fakes*,[10] Umberto Eco points out: 'What radio and television are today, we know – incontrollable plurality of messages that each individual uses to make up his own composition with the remote-control switch.' But 'what is a mass medium today? A TV program – that too, surely'. But isn't it also:

> the newspaper advertisement . . . the Polo shirt [imprinted or embroidered with the logo of the producers]? Here we

have not one but two, three, perhaps more mass media, acting through different channels . . . And at this point who is sending the message? . . . There is no longer Authority, all on its own (and how consoling it was!) . . . Power is elusive, and there is no longer any telling where the 'plan' comes from [a 'plan' is surely there] but it is no longer intentional, and therefore it cannot be criticized with the traditional criticism and intentions.

Eco penned the quoted essay back in 1983. No wonder Radio and TV figure still as the prime characters in the mass media drama. Had the author lived long enough to update the essay to match the wi-fi, digitalized era of the World Wide Web, the Internet and pocketsize, touch-screen computers, he would surely have many more questions to ask and much graver trouble in answering them unambiguously. Once upon a time, it was hoped that information would map the world legibly and equip the laid-up roads with firm and solid, storm and flood-resistant signposts at the crossings. Its business is now to render the signposts eminently mobile by perching them on well-lubricated castors, easily pushed and sent rolling with one touch of one finger on the user-friendly monitor's 'delete' key – a facility particularly welcome and ever more frequently and gratefully used by internauts in search of 'comfort zones' inside the infuriatingly yet hopelessly turbulent, notoriously chaotic and confusing world. With this facility included in every personal computer, decomposing messages from the multi-channel noises comes to its owner as easily as composing them – though with both cases remaining similarly risky and 'until further notice' only. In a world supplied with such equipment, the maps fed into sat-navs need to be updated ever more often while most drivers risk finding them nevertheless grossly outdated and liable to lead them astray.

Paradoxically, the past provides a most convenient, and in many ways most attractive and tempting, building site for such comfort zones. Paradoxically – because it is believed to be a warehouse of irrevocable *faits accomplis*, interspersed with vacuums that are impossible to fill retrospectively – it ought in principle to limit severely the freedom of message composers and so gravely restrict the number of conceivable choices; were he or she to treat seriously and obey in good faith Leopold von Ranke's demand to study events of the past 'as they actually happened', many a returnee would be bound to give up his or her preferential choices. Worse still: given the practical un-finishability of Ranke-style historiographic inquiries, and so the endemic un-decidability of interpretational *querelles*, they may be induced to abandon the very hope of constructing a defensible 'comfort zone' out of the 'facts of the past'. This is not, however, likely to happen.

On the contrary, the irreducible obscurities of the past, the multiplicity of interpretations to which every selection of past events is amenable, and the resulting incompleteness and contentiousness of any attempt at a comprehensive and coherent narrative of the 'as things actually happened' sort may be a nasty irritant for a professional historian – but are precisely the advantages of the past when attracting people seeking defensible trench lines for their faith. The very un-resolvability of disagreements, impossibility of submitting the narratives to the ultimate test of truth, allow the faithful to hold fast to their conviction, however weighty the arguments raised by their antagonists might be.

In matters of faith, the purpose of debate is not consent, but showing the adversary to be incurably deaf and blind to 'the facts of the matter', and fatally addicted to malice aforethought. The verdict of ill intentions makes the proofs of one's own veracity redundant. Listening to the adversary is strongly un-recommended, empathy with the adversary is a fatal, all but suicidal, blunder, and 'when you are arguing against the other side, do not use their language', as George Lakoff (praised by Geoffrey Nunberg of the University of California for combining 'a linguist's ear for the subtleties of language with an understanding of the complexities of modern politics' in the latest (2014) version of Lakoff's *Don't Think of an Elephant* study, described by George Akerlof, Nobel Prize-winner in economics, as 'a work of genius'[11]) warns current and aspiring actors on the political scene or in its wings (p. 1). Contrary to the myth widely accepted by political actors, the users of communication channels plug their ears to messages appealing to their self-interest whenever those messages come from senders branded a priori as 'they': a priori sworn enemies of 'us. Listening to such messages would be a betrayal of "our" identity, threatening to weaken our resolve and sap the very foundation of the world to which we belong: *our* world.' 'People do not necessarily vote in their self-interest', Lakoff warns: 'They vote their identity. They vote their values. They vote for who they identify with. They may identify with their self-interest. That can happen. It is not that people never care about their self-interest. But they vote their identity. And if their identity fits their self-interest, they will

vote for that. It is important to understand that point'
(p. 17).

Otherwise, he adds, 'facts go in and then they go right
back out. They are not heard, or they are not accepted
as facts, or they mystify us. Why would anyone have
said that? Then we label the fact as irrational, crazy,
or stupid' – and by proxy we extend that label to those
who said it, 'in case they did not carry that label before
speaking' (p. 16).

Another explanation of the astonishing phenomenon
of sacrificing one's self-interest for the sake of cling-
ing to one's identity comes from Friedrich Nietzsche:
'Simply the inherited feeling of being a higher being,
with higher pretensions, makes one rather cold, and
leaves the conscience in peace.' And so 'egoism is not
evil' – it is just that the fact that 'the other suffers *must
be learned*; and it can never be learned completely'.
What follows is that:

> Malice does not aim at the suffering of the other in and of
> itself, but rather at our own enjoyment . . . Every instance
> of teasing shows that it gives us a pleasure to release our
> power on the other person and experience an enjoyable
> feeling of superiority . . . [What is at stake is one's] own
> superiority, which can be *discovered* only in the suffering
> of the other, in teasing, for example.[12]

Praised as he was for exceptional sensitivity to
prodromal, embryonic, inchoate, still formless subter-
ranean axiological trends in European (Western? Global
in its potential and in the process of becoming?) culture,
Nietzsche did not – could not – visualize a world containing a Facebook, a Twitter, a MySpace, a LinkedIn: a
world in which acts of creating or breaking inter-human

bonds, inclusion of others in or exclusion of them from the *Lebenswelt*, and all in all drawing the frontlines between 'us' and 'them', have been rendered instantaneous and reduced to a few moves of a finger. They turned accessible to everyone and at any time. In such a world, the possibilities of 'releasing power on the other person', and so the occasions to relish 'an enjoyable feeling of one's own superiority', become boundless and all but infinite. They also move out from the realm of moral evaluation into the space of aesthetics – the field, as Kant suggested, of disinterested, non-instrumental and autotelic experience. The main – all too often, the sole – role assigned to the other(s) on whom aspersions are showered is to quench one's own thirst for superiority. In the case of digitalized obloquy, calumny and defamation, the seductiveness of such a method of seeking ego-gratification grows immensely – thanks to its anonymity and its being, by and large, un-indictable and so remaining (hopefully) un-impeachable, as well as staying unpunished.

In a culture in which, as Lindy West reports in the 11 March 2016 issue of the *New York Times*, 'some people believe that it's worse to be called racist than to be racist', many people are likely to perceive such digitalized facility as a Godsent gift. During one of the numerous crowded gatherings of enthusiastic supporters of Donald Trump, a Ms Kemper ('blazing, passionate, incredulous') confides: 'I think this country better go back to some of those values. Some of the values my parents grew up with, my grandparents grew up with'; 'Whatever was wrong, they could point it out and tell you.'[13] By being voiced in public using no more gadgets than a mundane microphone, with no beating about the bush and with face uncovered, thoughts that had been half-clandestinely honed and groomed in the privacy of talking to a smart phone or touching the keyboard of a tablet, the key to endearing Mr Trump to the online-formatted nation was turned.

Mr Trump is but one specimen (albeit one leading in spectacularity and notoriety) of the large and growing category of the 'politicians of anger', as the title of an article published by the Harvard professor Dani Rodrik, in *Social Europe*,[14] suggests they are. 'The conflicts between a hyper-globalized economy and social cohesion are real', observes the author; 'Two types of political cleavage are exacerbated in the process: an identity cleavage, revolving around nationhood, ethnicity, or religion, and an income cleavage, revolving around social class. Populists derive their appeal from one or the other of these categories . . . In both cases, there is a clear 'other' toward which anger can be directed.'; 'The appeal of populists is that they give voice to the anger of the excluded.'

Under such circumstances, keeping anger perpetually smouldering and glowing offers the best recipe for the populists' success: anger of the excluded and abandoned is a uniquely rich ore from which constant supplies of profuse political capital can be extracted – and given that the solutions for whose promotion that capital is used tend to be 'misleading and often dangerous', there is little or no chance of the supplies of that ore becoming exhausted in the foreseeable future. Rather like the corpses burnt in the crematoria in Auschwitz or Treblinka, supplies of that ore don't need an extra fuel; constantly smouldering anger delivers its own heat.

All the same, to many of the degraded and abandoned

people in this world marked by a swelling abyss between
the free-floating global elite and locals fixed to the
ground, angry and horrified as they can't help but be
at the prospect of exclusion, the 'back to tribes' policies with their calls to build walls, tighten borders and
extradite the aliens augur (as Vadim Nikitin suggested[15])
'shelter and compassion, not hatred and division'. What
they in fact portend is shelter for some (for 'us'), hatred
for some others (for 'them'). Pugnacity and astringency,
together with the bleak and bitter, raw-and-rough practices of tribes, wear the mask of shielding, safeguarding
'communities'. And communities – like the security they
temptingly, even if deceptively, promise – are (to use
Lakoff's language) Janus-faced 'frames': freedom from
trouble bedaubed all over one – smiling – face, with the
threat of demotion and exclusion on the other, sullen
and dreary. What the security metaphor ('security as
containment – keeping the evildoers out'[16]) brings to
mind, as Lakoff suggests, are the ideas of securing (our)
borders, keeping them and (their) weapons out of our
airports, having marshals on planes.

Most experts are of the opinion that all such measures are bound to remain ineffective; a smart terrorist
can penetrate any security system. As far as popular –
native, as distinct from alien – impressions and creeds
go, such expert opinion matters little, however. What
does matter is the power the frame holds on our mental
activities: 'Frames are mental structures that shape the
way we see the world. As a result, they shape the goals
we seek, the plans we make, the way we act, and what
counts as a good or bad outcome of our actions.'[17] And
what the frame of 'community' shapes is a vision of the
world and of our mode of being in the world which tie

integration closely together with separation: cosiness of home with the unhomeliness of exteriority; friendliness inside with estrangement, suspiciousness and watchfulness outside. That vision and that mode are nowadays epitomized in the phenomenon of nationalism.

*

Anthony D. Smith, widely recognized as the leading British authority on nations and nationalism, asks: 'Why have the fires of ferocious nationalism been rekindled, not forty years after they were thought to have burnt themselves out in the *Götterdämmerung* of the Third Reich?' – only to follow that question right away with the observation that 'the fires of nationalism were never quenched, only temporarily screened from view by our guilty realization of their awful consequences.[18] Even in the West, ethnic nationalism survived under a thin veneer of social democracy and liberalism', which leads him to a conclusion that 'the nation and nationalism remain the only realistic basis for a free society of states in the modern world'.

We may say, however, that, as far as the 'frames' of nation, state and territorial sovereignty go, they all rest on the firm, and anything but shrinking or fading, experience of living in a world criss-crossed by borders, punctuated by border posts and manned by immigration control officers. It is, I suggest, this experience that provides the raw stuff from which a wide range of variations on the theme of 'us' and 'them' (or, in pragmatic terms, of integration through separation, and separation through integration) is developed. As Anthony D. Smith observes, 'any cultural element can function as a diacritical mark or badge of the nation – though it may make a considerable difference which is chosen in certain circumstances' (p. 150) – some scholars going as far as denying the very possibility of a 'consistent doctrine of nationalism' (p. 149); Smith himself would have stopped well before embarking that far – but all the same he selects as the sole common feature of all nationalisms 'an ideological movement for the attainment and maintenance of autonomy, unity and identity on behalf of a population deemed by some of its members to constitute a "nation"' (pp. 149–50).

In his magnum opus quoted here, Smith mentioned the great Norwegian anthropologist Fredrik Barth only once – and this in a chapter dedicated to 'modernist fallacies' in the approaches to the national question. Without engaging in extensive argument, he dismisses Barth's insistence on the priority of social boundaries over cultural difference, even if acquitting him, conditionally, of the charge of falling headlong into the 'social-boundary fallacy'; Barth 'is not pure instrumentalism', Smith concedes, in as far as he believes 'that ethnic identities are in some sense pre-existing and "out there"' (p. 164) – whatever 'being out there' may mean.

In fact, the school created and led by Barth, and with whose essential tenets I am in full accord, stood out by treating the attention to cultural difference as a derivative of social boundary practices – as the very title of his fundamental study signals. In his own words, Barth's approach differed from other approaches by 'attempting to explore the different processes that seem to be involved in generating and maintaining ethnic groups' 'rather than working through a typology of forms of ethnic groups and relations'; and by shifting 'the focus of investigation from internal constitution and history of separate groups to ethnic boundaries and boundary maintenance'.[19] Having pointed out that, among students of the national issue, 'the sharing of a common culture is generally given central importance', Barth averred that 'much can be gained by regarding this very important feature as an implication or result, rather than a primary and definitional characteristic of ethnic group organization' (p. 11); 'The critical focus of investigation from this point of view becomes the ethnic *boundary* that defines the group, not the cultural stuff that it encloses' (p. 15). In Barth's view, which I fully share, casting others as 'culturally alien, derivative of assumed recognition of limitations to shared understandings', implies 'a restriction of interaction to sectors of assumed common understanding and mutual interest' (ibid.).

In the thirteenth, 2006 printing of his classic *Nations and Nationalism since 1780: Programme, Myth, Reality*, Eric Hobsbawm notes that, 'since the book was first published in early 1990, more new nation-states have been formed, or are in the process of formation, than at any time in the century . . . All states are today officially "nations", all political agitations are apt to be against foreigners, whom practically all states hurry and seek to keep out'.[20]

'They' can be, must be, blamed for all the grievances, uncertainties and disorientations which so many of us feel after forty years of the most rapid and profound upheavals in human life in recorded history. And who are 'they'? Obviously, and virtually by definition, those who are 'not us' – the strangers who, by their very alienness, are enemies . . . If the foreigners with their knavish tricks did not exist, it would be necessary to invent them. But at the end of our millennium they rarely have to be invented: they are universally present and recognizable within our cities, as public dangers and agents of pollution, universally present, beyond our borders and control, but hating and conspiring against us. (p. 174)

Hobsbawm stops well short of declaring the explosion of nationalism, bent as it is on adding new politically autonomous units to those into which planetary humanity has already been split, to be a natural, there-is-no-alternative product of the 'objective' law of history – or an inalienable feature of the species-wide mode of being. Quite the opposite: he asserts repeatedly that this explosion is in the last account a consequence of human choice – and, as is the nature of choices, it could be different: 'The simplest way to describe the apparent explosion of separatism in 1988–92 is . . . as "unfinished business of 1918–21"' (p. 165); 'the definition of "the nation" and its aspirations which, paradoxically, Lenin shared with Woodrow Wilson, automatically created the fracture lines along which multinational units . . . were to break, just as the colonial frontiers of 1880–1950 were to form the state frontiers of post-colonial states, there being no others available' (p. 166). In other words: *it was a series of man-made choices that led to a situation of no choice.*[21]

There was, as a matter of fact, another choice, before the victors of the World War who had gathered in Versailles resolved to accept the territorial separation and sovereignty of each nation as a universal, globally binding principle. It was hoped at that time that the world order built on this principle would make the recently finished war the last in the long row of gory sequences of inter-ethnic strife: a war that would prevent all future wars (as it happened, the resolution inspired by Woodrow Wilson paved the way to by far the bloodiest war in the world's history).

That other choice was broached in the areas of Europe called by Hannah Arendt 'belts of mixed population'. For centuries, numerous ethnic, religious and linguistic categories lived there in close proximity, interspersed between each other; were the Versailles formula (arousing from the Westphalian settlement of 1648) to be applied there, it would be anything but clear which of the numerous languages, religions or ethnic cultural lores deployed in a given territory should set the standard binding the population of the prospective political unit. The odds were that each project would be hotly contested. To quote again Ernest Gellner's study of *Nations and Nationalism*:

> It is customary to comment on the strength of nationalism. This is an important mistake, though readily understandable since, whenever nationalism has taken root, it has tended to prevail with ease over other modern ideologies.
>
> Nevertheless, the clue to the understanding of nationalism is its weakness at least as much as its strength. It was the dog who failed to bark who provided the vital clue for Sherlock Holmes. The numbers of potential nationalisms who failed to bark is far, far larger than those which did, though *they* have captured all our attention. (p. 42)

Gellner's 'rough calculation' (p. 44) 'gives us only one effective nationalism for ten potential ones! . . . For every effective nationalism, there are *n* potential ones . . . which fail to activate their potential nationalism, which do not even try' (though, let me comment more than three decades after Gellner's calculation was conducted, the value of '*n*' has been all but shrinking – and all around the globe, even if with varying speed). With globalization of interdependence turning all, or at least an overwhelming majority, of the 'territorial sovereignties', gradually yet steadily, into illusion, the criteria deployed for granting the right to territorial political separation are also gradually yet steadily made less and less demanding – a circumstance which constitutes itself as one of the most powerful factors boosting the 'back to tribes' tendencies.

In one of the most prominent 'belts of mixed population' was the Austro-Hungarian Empire; and it is there where the alternative choice was broached and thoroughly ventilated, mostly in the social-democratic sector of the political spectrum. That alternative was a cultural, but not territorial and not state-political, autonomy of ethnicities. To put it in the nutshell, the choice in question boiled down to the mutual separation of the 'national problem' from that of territory, followed by its association with the 'personality principle' (national self-identification is a matter of personal choice, not of administrative assignment by the state). The most representative of the series of publications promoting that choice was perhaps Otto Bauer's 1907 *Die Nationalitätenfrage und die Sozialdemokratie.*[22]

All the same, the proliferation of new territorially separate divisions – sharing, however, in the same inclination to be 'apt to be against foreigners' – is by no means a new phenomenon; in fact, as Hobsbawm reminds us, it was already noted by Georg Simmel: 'It may even be a piece of political wisdom to see to it that there be some enemies in order for the unity of the members to be effective and for the group to remain conscious of the unity as its vital interest.'[23] Indeed, as all three legs (military, economic and cultural) of the tripod of sovereignties on which the political sovereignty of the territorial nation-state perches are crippled, diluted and washed out by the rising tides of globalization of finances, commodity trade and information, this might turn out to be the sole 'political wisdom' sought, found and applied by rising numbers of actual and aspiring political leaders who have little to offer to their electors except 'consciousness of the unity' rooted in a distant and murky past, but resoundingly confirmed by the crafty schemes and underhand plots concocted by 'them' – the aliens, the foreigners, the strangers crowding at our door and in our midst. As I've already tried to explain in an interview conducted by Brad Evans for the *New York Times*' 'The Stone', when asked 'do you think the current refugee crises engulfing Europe represent yet another chapter in the history of flight from persecution or is there something different taking place here?': 'It is yet another chapter' indeed, though as is the habit with successive chapters, something will be added to the contents of their predecessors.

*

In the modern era, massive migration is not a novelty; nor is it a sporadic event prompted by an extraordinary, one-off concatenation of circumstances. It is in fact a constant, steady effect of the modern mode of life, with its perpetual preoccupation with order-building and economic progress – two qualities that act in their effects as factories of 'redundant people': of people locally unemployable or intolerable and therefore forced to seek shelter or more promising life opportunities away from their homes.

True, the prevalent itineraries of migrants change their direction following the spread of the modern way of life from Europe, its place of origin, to the rest of the globe. As long as Europe remained the only 'modern' continent on the planet, its redundant population kept being unloaded onto the still 'premodern' lands – recycled into colonist settlers, soldiers or members of the colonial administration (up to 60 million Europeans are believed to have left Europe for the two Americas, Africa or Australia during the heyday of colonial imperialism). Starting from the middle of the twentieth century, the trajectory of migration, however, took a U-turn: from being centrifugal to centripetal in relation to Europe. This time over, however, migrants carried no arms; neither did they aim at the conquest of the land of their destination. The migrants of the post-colonial era have been and still are exchanging their inherited ways of eking out existence, now destroyed by the triumphant modernization promoted by their former colonizers, for the chance of building a nest in the gaps in those colonizers' domestic economies.

On top of that, however, there is a rising volume of people forced out from their homes by the dozens of civil wars, ethnic and religious conflicts and sheer banditry in the territories the colonizers left behind in the nominally sovereign, artificially concocted 'states' with little prospects of stability but enormous arsenals of weaponry – of arms seeking targets – supplied by their former colonial masters. The seemingly prospectless destabilization of the Middle-Eastern area in the aftermath of miscalculated, foolishly myopic and admittedly abortive policies and military ventures of Western powers is the most noted, but by no means the only, case in this category. In fact, a huge part of Africa – the belt between the two tropics, Cancer and Capricorn – has been transformed into a mass refugee factory.

Michel Agier, the foremost researcher of the nature and consequences of mass migration, warns that current estimates presage 1 billion 'displaced persons' in the next forty years: 'After globalization of capitals, commodities and images, the time for globalization of *humanity* has finally arrived [italics added]'.[24] But the displaced are people with no place of their own and no place to be legitimately claimed; as Agier points out, the travel itself, conducted with no clear point of arrival, makes 'no-place' their indefinitely durable place: they, so to speak, lack place in the shared world (pp. 20–1). But these 'no-places' of refugees (as, for instance, the railway stations of Rome and Milan, or Belgrade Central Park) are in our – the lucky 'natives' free to travel by choice instead of by blows of ill fate – neighbourhoods. Finding oneself face-to-face with such 'no-places', instead of watching them at a safe distance on TV screens, is a shocking experience. It brings the worldwide turbulence with all its demons, literally, home. Globalization with all its unsavoury side-effects stays no longer 'out there', but down here, on the street where we live – or many others which we need to pass through on the way to our job or in our children's school.

The point, though, is that keeping global misfortune effectively away by fencing oneself off in the hoped-for security of home territory is no more likely than avoiding the consequences of a nuclear war by hiding in a family shelter. Global problems call for global solutions; nothing else can chase them away. Purely and simply, leaving the problem to fester, on condition that it does so elsewhere instead of in our own backyard, just won't do. The *radical*, ultimate cure stays beyond the reach of any single – however big and powerful – country: even beyond an assembly of countries, such as the European Union – whether we confine 'the migrants' to camps built in Europe, Africa or Asia, or let them vanish in the waters of the Mediterranean or the Pacific.

In the last account, tribes (be they 'primeval', 'primitive', as they appeared to the elitist-intellectual promoters of nations much as the old-style socialists appeared to Karl Marx as 'utopian', an offspring of centuries-long self-deception overdue for profound revision and rehashing by a scientific critique – or dressed in their 'new and improved', since 'rationalized', garb of 'nations') are products of the human, all-too-human, need to cut down the incomprehensible and so disabling complexity of the shared human existential condition to a dimension graspable by human senses and intelligible: one of 'standing to reason'.

Since the birth of the human species, this reduction was accomplished by dividing the world of humans into 'us' and 'them': those inside the universe of moral obligation or those cast outside. As Levinas suggested, such a division was (and may well remain) an indispensable part and parcel of the continuous effort to make the mode of 'being in society' underpinned by the 'absolute responsibility *for* the other' the principle and the urge underlying *all* human coexistence. Divisions are the necessary tools in that job, in so far as the principle of absolute and unconditional responsibility for all and any other humans is fashioned to the measure of saints, not the creatures well short of saintliness that most of us are – and are most likely, perhaps bound, to remain for the duration.

Thus far, two parallel pressures have influenced the meanders of that job's twists and turns. One: the quantitative growth in the volume of 'us', from the hordes of hunter/gatherers to the present-day 'imagined totalities' of the nation-states. The other: the 'civilizing process' – 'softening of mores' inside that constantly expanding habitat of 'us' – forced therefore to admit, adopt and absorb an unstoppably growing number of strangers – to replace the impulse of rejection, the instinctual pugnacity and unmitigated hostility to strangers, with 'civil inattention' and/or with verbal-only, symbolic warfare. Such pressures came, however, nowhere near to changing the rules of the thousands-of-years-old 'us vs them' game. The current massive influx of strangers, still far from finished and in all likelihood bound to rise rather than diminish in volume, has caught us as unprepared as were those tribes to which we strive to return.

In the 14 January issue of the *New York Times*, Roger Cohen[25] recalls that between the 1880s and 1924 the US allowed in 4 million Italian immigrants. He quotes Leon Wieseltier of the Brookings Institution: 'We got Enrico Fermi, Frank Sinatra, Joe DiMaggio, Antonin Scalia – and Al Capone. Who in their right mind would suggest that the Italian immigration was not a great blessing for our country?' Cohen goes on:

President Obama showcased a Syrian immigrant, Refaai Hamo, during the State of the Union address as evidence of 'our diversity and our openness' . . . But given the degree of openness America has offered Syrian refugees over close to five years of war in which a quarter of a million people have been killed, this political choreography qualified as a serious chutzpah.

America accepted during that five-year-long period about 2,500 Syrian refugees ('roughly 0.06 percent of the 4.4 million Syrians who fled the country'). Hamo, therefore, 'might better have been offered as a symbol of the closing of the American mind' – a closing, let me add, that itself is eminently fit to be showcased as evidence of running, at an accelerating pace, back to tribes.

A few days earlier, on 8 January, the same newspaper informed, in its editorial:

> Since New Year's, the administration has been sending agents into homes to make an example of the offenders and to defend the principle of a secure border. A president who spoke so movingly about the violent gun deaths of children here has taken on the job of sending mothers and children on one-way trips to the deadliest countries in our hemisphere [Honduras, Guatemala and El Salvador]. Mothers and children who pose no threat, actual or imaginable, to our security.[26]

From all the manifold historical departures, the propensity and propulsion to divide humans (whether distant and inaccessible or within reach) into 'us' and 'them' has heretofore emerged unharmed – even if the behavioural patterns they design and promote may alter. As long as 'humanity' remains a phantom, an un-intelligible entity, mentally and pragmatically unassimilable (recall Ulrich Beck's acid assessment of the state of our cosmopolitan consciousness lagging far behind the cosmopolitan realities of our present-day life), the search for identity – that is, the tackling of internal and external pressures to trace and fix one's own positioning in the world populated by others, as well as the necessity to subject one's choice to the recognition and approval of others – will continue to demand a reference point; 'like' vs 'unlike', 'belonging' vs 'alienness', etc. – in short, *us* vs *them* – are (and threaten to remain for a long time to come) indispensable tools in the job of self-identification: for 'us' to exist, 'they', the 'not-us', must exist or be conjured up, or in the last resort fantasized (and they are indeed present, invented, appointed or imagined, in each and every variety, or stage, of its performance). The growing size of (at least some of) the groups with which and in opposition to which people tend to identify, as well as the mellowing ('civilizing') of the interactions of the insiders (or at least some of them), are but changes in quantity, not quality – in form, not in function.

*

For tribes and for nations alike, identity (whether consciously elected or tacitly, passively bestowed and assumed at birth) carried stern demands: 'belonging' tended to wear a fully and truly 'life and death' character – non-negotiable and unlimited. 'Sacrificing my life for the benefit of the group' was as much an integral part of the mode of life in tribes as it became the postulated ultimate test of belonging in the case of the 'imagined totalities' of nation-states – the modern formations retaining that one maxim while refuting and rejecting a plethora of other items in the heritage of that tribal past that it has renounced wholesale. That grim and cruel maxim has, in turn, been all but withdrawn, or died down, once it had become redundant – even bothersome and counter-productive – as a result of (and in close synchronization with) the replacement of a warfare relying on mass conscription and mass levy by technologically sophisticated operations of small professional armies, as well as of the emancipation of economic exploitation from its past close links with territorial conquest.

The story of the 'away from the tribes' episode, and even more of the presently on-going 'back to tribes' process, would, however, be grossly incomplete if the recent informatics / digital cultural revolution failed to be included in their pictures. By itself, the entry of digital informatics into the daily life of a large and fast-growing sector of humanity is solely a new chapter in the history of technology; and yet its almost universal availability and fully and truly 'de-territorialized' mobility, not synchronized with the movement of our bodies (and becoming, in effect, for most of us, an undetached, and for all practical intents and purposes inseparable, extension of our bodies – a quality neither achieved nor as much as contemplated, let alone attempted, by any other technical appliance), has thoroughly revised our set of options and created an awesome multitude of never-before-faced, but now realistic, responses to familiar stimuli – while also acquiring the capability of generating a host of quite novel stimuli previously un-confronted, and releasing impulses and actions previously untried and untested. According to the logic of instrumental rationality in reverse ('Let me know to what uses this appliance can be put' and 'Because this is what it can do, I'll do this!'), the new opportunities, possibilities and chances lead to the re-evaluation of the relative attractiveness of behavioural patterns open to choice, and by proxy revolutionize the probabilities of these, rather than those, lines of conduct being selected from among alternatives.

Electronic media are, however, neutral about the way that logic of instrumental rationality needs to, shall or will be deployed by their users. The new media facilitate (and by the same token favour) the selection of cultural omnivorousness as much as they do a stringent while whimsical selectiveness in information-gathering, network-building and communication – all three being the most common functions/uses of those media. They encourage openness and Hans Gadamer's 'fusion of horizons' no more (though no less either) than they do the hermetically locking oneself off from everything loftily dismissed for being found unwieldy, inconvenient and discomforting. Both the multiplication of inputs and their strict limitation become that much easier than ever before to achieve (and than they still are inside the offline universe). They are capable of *facilitating* human choices, of *manipulating* their respective probabilities – but most certainly not of *determining* those choices, let alone of guaranteeing their consistent and steadfast pursuit; seeing them all the way through to their implementation and adoption of a shape chiming in with their original design.

3
Back to Inequality

In his novel *Sybil, or Two Nations*, published in 1845, Disraeli put in the lips of a working-class radical, Walter Gerard, the following statement:

> Two nations; between whom there is no intercourse and no sympathy; who are as ignorant of each other's habits, thoughts, and feelings, as if they were dwellers in different zones, or inhabitants of different planets; who are formed by a different breeding, are fed by a different food, are ordered by different manners, and are not governed by the same laws.

On which pronouncement, one of the main characters of the novel, Charles Egremont, commented: 'The rich and the poor'.[1]

Speaking as a vice-presidential nominee to the Democratic National Convention held almost 160 years later, on 28 July 2004, Senator John Edwards restated the 'two nations' thesis, coining a new name for the division between the two: *the haves and the have nots*.[2] Edwards pointed out that: 'the truth is, we still live in a country where there are two different Americas . . . One, for all of those people who have lived the American dream and don't have to worry, and another for most Americans, everybody else who struggle to make ends meet every single day. It doesn't have to be that way.'[3]

Between themselves, the quoted assessments of society's current condition and realistic prospects as well as of the challenges it faced at the time the assessments were made, go a long way towards unravelling the roots of the phenomenon of retrotopia. Most of those nearly 160 years dividing the two assessments were devoted to efforts to make Disraeli's verdict null and void: to the elimination of poverty. At some point, during the 'glorious thirty' post-war years, the rampant inequality cutting society into two nations was commonly viewed as earmarked for extinction, and whatever had been left of its inheritance was seen as a temporary irritant. As Michal Kalecki observed in an essay under the title 'Political Aspects of Full Employment', published in the *Political Quarterly* of 1943[4] on the threshold of the 'social state' era,[5] 'a solid majority of economists is now of the opinion that, even in a capitalist system, full employment may be secured by a government spending programme'.[6] And a similar majority of the learned/informed opinion supported the view that the way out from the unacceptable level of inequality – that is, the kind of inequality known to sediment a large layer of the population living below the poverty line – leads through providing jobs to all with adequate living wages to all. It was also widely believed that the role of initiator, designer and executive in the last battle against the abomination of uncontrolled inequality that splits society into a nation of the rich and a nation of the

Retrotopia

poor is to be played by governments. By itself, without governmental supervision and monitoring, the economy wouldn't deliver the desired effects. War against poverty needs to be waged and conducted by political organs deploying political weapons.

For a few decades, that conviction steered close to the status of being axiomatic, as it was shared by the whole political spectrum of the time; fully and truly, it could be presented as located 'beyond left and right' division – even if different sectors of the spectrum joined in to share the same view for different reasons: the capitalists because of the seemingly unbreakable mutuality of dependence between capital and labour (labour depending on capital for its living, but capital, in the days of the 'solid' phase of modernity, depending as much on labour – and mostly local labour – for its reproduction and to retain its wealth-producing capacity). Labour shared that view – due to being doomed to reiterate the buying–selling transactions with capital for the foreseeable time to come, and therefore eager to create and maintain the conditions likely to raise its value and attractiveness for its prospective capitalist buyers. Finally, the same view was held by the state, whose function, as Jürgen Habermas explained in his study *Legitimationsprobleme im Spätkapitalismus*, published (after the habit of the Owl of Minerva, known to spread its wings at dusk) in 1973 – that is, at the very end of that capital–labour 'mutual dependence' period – was to assure the perpetuation of the buying–selling capital–labour transactions, thus obliging it to keep labour in a condition that made it an attractive commodity to its prospective buyers, by subsidizing education, healthcare, provision of decent accommodation and whatever other expenditures such

88

an endeavour required – in other words, sharing in the costs of reproduction of good-quality labour to enable capitalists to pay its market price. With the regular successful meetings of capital eager to buy labour and labour keen to sell it thereby assured, the state of affairs looked to each of the three players as a good – or at least better than its conceivable alternatives – solution. Were they asked, all three would perhaps opine of that solution as Winston Churchill did, allegedly, of democracy (as the worst political regime except for all the others).

The question of how it happened that this honeymoon – or, more to the point, this armistice between capital and labour, presided over and serviced by the capitalist state – ground to an abrupt halt is still relatively fresh (but for how much longer?) in the public memory and too hotly debated to allow definite summarizing. Many reasons for that collapse have been (and go on being) suggested, and many culprits named – but the unilateral cancellation by the bosses of the mutuality of the capital–labour dependency, triggered by globalization but zealously aided and abetted by the state dismantling, one by one, constraints imposed on the capitalists' greed and the framework and fabric of its victims' defensibility, seems to be the prime contender for utmost pride of place.

*

As Émile Durkheim convincingly argued, once the socially constructed and codified norms equipped with ultimate authority, effective sanctions and so a binding power, start to lose their hold over human choices or explicitly reject them, people who used to be subject to their coercive impact not so much acquire freedom of self-assertion as turn into serfs of their instinct and impulses (norms imposed by the society are, after the pattern of Hobbes' Leviathan, people's sole effective defence against their own – base and destructive, all but suicidal – predilections and unbridled emotions). It looks like – at least in the case of the capitals let off the leash under the rule of Ronald Reagan, Margaret Thatcher and their numerous followers and imitators – Durkheim's sombre foreboding came true: all the more so for the fact that the new order of things to which they played midwife affected the two different sides in the conflict of interests in radically divergent ways. The release from normative regulation was, to say the least, one-sided; the first use to which capitals emancipated from politically designed and imposed norms put their new freedoms, was to wrap labour tightly in a dense net of newly promulgated legal limitations, while stripping it of whatever decision-making capability it had managed to win in the years of reciprocal capital–labour interdependence. As to the on-going overhaul of the capital–state relationships, it is enough to note the enthusiasm with which stock exchanges greet successive rounds of massive redundancy, and their horror at the sight of the state contemplating a rise in taxes and/or increased social expenditures in order to mitigate the social damage caused – a horror to which globetrotting finances are prompt to react by blackmailing the guilty state back into obedience – from which, it seems, it dared (thoughtlessly, if not criminally, as we are told) to veer. The recent (and still, at the moment of my writing, far from finished) Golgotha of Greece put that state of affairs, with the ardent help of the global mass media, on spectacular display – though it ought to be viewed as,

by intention, a 'guide to the perplexed' aspiring to pru-
dence, rather than as a one-off, let alone an exceptional
and self-inflicted calamity.

Branko Milanovic, who, according to the *New York
Magazine*[7] 'has spent decades studying income inequality' (as far back as when 'even the word inequality was
not politically acceptable, because it seemed like something wild or socialist or whatever'), puts the results
of all that in the nutshell: 'It's a perfect storm . . . It's
forgotten by the Establishment in the rich countries that
you have to pay attention to the losers.' 'More and more
people in the top one percent are rich, both in terms of
the capital they receive a return on *and* their labour. It's
very new. You don't have the old-fashioned thing with
only capitalists and workers. Now the richest people
have both kinds of income' – which suggests that those
who are less than 'the richest' are doubly deprived,
having less and less of both and falling in danger of
losing each. Politically, this means that, instead of 'par-
ticipatory democracy', what 'we now see it's really much
more one-dollar-one-vote than one-person-one vote'.

The matter is no longer contentious. Whatever measure of inequality is preferred by the economists of one
school or another, it brings strikingly consensual results:
inequality is growing – from the turn of the century, the
added value in economic growth almost exclusively goes
to the richest 1 per cent of the population (some speak
already of 0.5 percent, even of 0.1 percent), while the
level of income and possessions of the rest of society is
either experiencing already, or expected to experience,
falling. The process took off at the very start of the new
millennium and acquired accelerating momentum with
the collapse of credit in 2007–8. Now, it has brought

us back to a situation the likes of which, in the so-called 'developed' countries of the northern hemisphere, haven't been encountered since the 1920s.

Here are just a few figures to 'career report' the present-day state of the rising societal and global inequalities. In the wealthiest country of the globe, the US, the wealthiest 160,000 families command between themselves as much capital as the poorest 145,000,000 families. The top 10 per cent of Americans own 86 per cent of American wealth, leaving to the other 90 per cent of the population 14 per cent of the national wealth to share. On the global dimension (according to the recent report by Credit Suisse), the bottom half of humanity (3.5 billion) has about 1 per cent of the world's total wealth – just as much as the 85 richest persons on earth.

*

Another 'back', then? Yes, but in this case un-planned, not articulated in political battles, not written on camp banners – neither postulated by any of the party-political programmes, nor explicitly advocated and fought for in either political or economic discourse; rather, an unanticipated – or at least not much thought about and not included in diagnoses or prognoses – incidental derivative of multiple forces let off the leash and uncontrolled.

And rather a long time had to pass before the take-off of the process was spotted – and an even longer time was needed for that spotting to make its way to the front pages of newspapers and into the speeches of leading mainstream politicians and public figures. This did not happen when the distance between the two – rich and poor – nations started to grow at a spectacular pace, even though all, or almost all, sectors of society seemed to follow the pattern which they had been trained to expect: a rise in their standard of living – big in good years, or at least mediocre or tiny, yet still palpable, in bad ones. The realization that some people 'up there' were getting better off much quicker than the rest of the people 'down here' was not enough to make the issue of inequality a 'number one problem' (or almost) of economic, political and social concern. What was needed for that feat to be accomplished was for the wealth and income of the increasingly limited fraction of the top and the well-being of the rapidly expanding rest to start moving in mutually opposite directions – as they have in several recent years. Only *that* change broke the habitual pattern by inflaming the slowly smouldering sadness of deprivation into red-hot anger kindled by the growing evidence of its relativity.

Scattered voices warning of the conflicts yet to come were promptly marginalized and effectively stifled and numbed by the chorus of opinion-making economists in the style of Friedrich Hayek (in the posthumously rehashed version of his legacy), Milton Friedman or Keith Joseph, eagerly composing odes of praise for the unerring 'invisible hand' of the market managing the stage on which 'each group has had to fight its own battles, often in open conflict with the demands of other groups'.[8] Amid the hubbub of Reagan/Thatcher's overhaul of political economy, the early warnings such as those coming, for instance, from Frank Parkin ('The awkward moment arrives when increased appetites must be satisfied from a cake that, for whatever reason, has failed to get bigger. At this point, expectations can only be met by the net transfer of resources from one group to another'[9]) or Robert Heilbroner (with 'the removal of the safety valve by which the deep tension between the claims of labour and property has been lessened in the past', a stationary capitalism is 'forced to confront the explosive issue of income distribution in a way that an expanding capitalism is spared'[10]) were hardly audible, let alone capable of catching and holding public attention.

*

The hardships people suffer tend to fall into two classes: habitual ones, suffered long enough to mesh into the daily reality and, by and large, to stop being seen as suffered unjustly and therefore calling for vengeance or rebellion; and new, sudden increments in the habitualized volume of hardship, sometimes minute by comparison with the 'normal', routine volume and intensity of suffering, but perceived as cases of injustice, and for that reason serving as a call to arms.

The concept of 'relative deprivation' and its intimately linked psycho-social consequences was coined and developed in somewhat differing ways by Robert K. Merton,[11] Walter Garrison Runciman[12] and Barrington Moore Jr.[13] They differed in their definition and evaluation of the phenomenon, but between themselves contributed significantly to the idea presently established in sociological practice that feelings of deprivation are relative, as they arise from a comparison to social norms that are neither absolute nor universal, differing from time to time and one place to another.[14] It is not the absolute, 'objective' volume and harshness of the suffered hardships that determines the discontent and dissent of the sufferers, leading eventually to protest and rebellion, but the deviation of the volume or intensity of the hardships they are forced to put up with from the distribution pattern of hardships between different sectors of society – the pattern tacitly accepted as 'normal' and thereby as legitimate.

A few examples: it was not the villein service demanded by the landlords – the non-remunerated labour on the lord's estate – however rigid and obtrusive that burdensome and oppressive duty might have been, that led mediaeval serfs to insurgency, but the act of raising the demands above the customary level. In modern times, trade unions were in the habit of calling their members out on strike when workers in the same trade and with the same level of skills received in another factory a wage rise which their members were refused. In our own times, young people from well-off families in the upper strata of society may, despite their inherited privileges, be prompted to rebel when, on entering the labour market, they find out that the plum jobs – and so, also, appropriately elevated social positions matching their education, ambition and expectation – are missing.

The overall message of the relative deprivation perspective and the studies it has begotten is that it is not the abstract standard of justice (and so an equally abstract definition of injustice coined by philosophers) that spurs the victims to rebellion – but a comparison with people around: contemporaries in 'real time', visible and palpable, familiar or heard of: those who furnish one's *Lebenswelt*. It is they who supply the 'reference groups', in juxtaposition with which the cases of dissent and rebellion under the banner of legitimate resistance to inequality tend to be articulated – or, rather, they are the pool from which the injured and offended select groups on whom to target their demands for compensation or lust for vengeance.

As Runciman spelled it out: 'relative deprivation should always be understood to mean a *sense* of deprivation; a person who is "relatively deprived" need not be "objectively deprived" in the more usual sense that he is demonstrably lacking something' (p. 12). Runciman quoted Alexis de Tocqueville to emphasize the divergence and far reaching mutual disconnect between inequality as the statistically graspable, objective, measurable distribution of material possessions, incomes, awarded prestige and their accoutrements, on one side, and the endemically subjective sense of deprivation suffered:

> It was precisely in those parts of France where there had been most improvement that popular discontent ran highest ... Patiently endured so long as it seemed beyond redress, a grievance comes to appear intolerable once the possibility of removing it crosses men's mind ... At the height of its power feudalism did not inspire so much hatred as it did on the eve of its eclipse. (p. 24)

And he finds support in Leonard Riessmann[15] for introducing yet another factor responsible for the above-mentioned divergence: 'those who had in fact been successful seemed to have had their aspirations heightened by success. Success, therefore, can itself provide the external stimulus by which comparisons are heightened, whereas those who are forced to adjust themselves to lesser achievement will reduce their aspirations in accordance with their experience.'

What follows from these observations is that, paradoxically, yesterday's success in upgrading one's social standing, when barred from being continued or repeated today, breeds and intensifies the grievance gestated by the perceived discrimination and adds animus to the urge to redress it. In a somewhat recycled form, this idea inspired the concept of the 'revolutions of rising expectations', widely used in theories of revolutions since the 1950s, and since 1969 associated mainly with James C. Davies' 'J-curve hypothesis'.[16] Davies suggested that the likelihood of violent revolutions derives its impetus from a downturn following a long period of rising expectations accompanied by a parallel increase in their satisfaction: 'When perceptions of need satisfaction decrease but expectations continue to rise, a widening gap is created between expectations and reality. That gap eventually becomes intolerable and sets the stage for rebellion against a social system that fails to fulfil its promises.'

*

The last quotation could have passed, almost word for word, as the description of our current condition. Are we, therefore, witnessing a 'revolutionary situation'? Let me add that our present-day condition chimes as well with Lenin's formula for the 'revolutionary situation' as a state of affairs in which the rulers can no longer rule in the way they did, while the ruled no longer wish to be ruled in the way they have been.

But, as in so many other cases of putative homogeneity covering up for the genuine heterogeneity, we may say that all similarities between the consequences likely to follow the apparently similar existential conditions then and now are here accidental: divergences overwhelm and dwarf the resemblances and congruities. In our thoroughly individualized and deregulated society of inherently ad hoc, volatile, temporary and fleeting, as well as fissiparous, alliances and coalitions of short and shortening life expectancy, and ever shrinking time–distance between usefulness and counter-productivity of undertakings in a society addicted to 'subsidiarizing' the tasks of societal politics to the level of individually run 'life politics', the hegemonic philosophy and the mode of life it prompts and gestates can be seen as a stratagem aimed at devaluing and denigrating human solidarity on anything other than the 'nearest and dearest' level. The probability of recasting the commonality of the existential condition into a sustained commonality of purpose and action is also minimal. Instead of gestating solidarity, the present-day existential condition, aided and abetted by the new managerial philosophy and the new strategy of domination, is a factory of mutual suspicion, antagonism of interests, rivalry and strife. As Paul Verhaeghe succinctly put it:

> Solidarity becomes an expensive luxury and makes way for temporary alliances, the main preoccupation always being to extract more profit from the situation than your competition. Social ties with colleagues weaken, as does emotional commitment to the enterprise or organisation. Bullying used to be confined to schools; now it is a common feature of the workplace. This is a typical symptom of the impotent venting their frustration on the weak – in psychology it's known as displaced aggression. There is a buried sense of fear, ranging from performance anxiety to a broader social fear of the threatening other.[17]

In a society in which 'the other' (*any* other) is either an already open-faced or unmasked or still undisclosed (and for that reason even more gruesome and frightening) threat, solidarity (and especially a committed solidarity of a sworn and covenanted kind) feels like a treacherous trap for the naïve, gullible, foolish and flippant. It 'stands to reason' (more precisely, to the *doxa* – substituted for reason by the currently hegemonic philosophy) to lean over backwards in order to avoid that trap. In the currency nowadays in circulation, solidarity does not pay. Instead of being a trustworthy asset, it is morbidly inclined to turn into liability. The stock exchanges of 'life politics' devalue Putnam's 'social capital' – while putting a premium on self-reference, self-concern and an anti-social edge of self-assertion.

It is not only 'social capital', however, that has fallen victim to the assets' rapidly ageing and outdated job performed by our individualized, privatized society, prominent as it is in ceding the tasks of Politics with a capital 'P' to individually designed, managed and monitored 'life politics'. 'Relative deprivation' may be suspected of sharing its fate. From a time- and space-bound sense of deprivation triggered by the seen or imagined group 'like us' being endowed with advantages denied to 'us', we move to a permanent, and sort of 'free-floating', ambience of deprivation, no longer fixed once and for all to a specific 'comparative group', but instead casting anchors randomly in any of the infinite number of harbours encountered along our life's itinerary.

With all varieties of human habitat on the planet open to visits and scrutiny, every human being's or human group's success is likely to be perceived as another annoying and exasperating case of my own deprivation and so to add to the warehouse of my grievances. In the individualized society, competition for the boons universally desired, yet stubbornly in short supply, cannot but be felt as a zero-sum game. Everybody's success feels like my defeat and seems to diminish my already meagre chances of 'moving up in the world'. One is therefore tempted to abandon the idea of the sentiment of 'relative deprivation' in favour of the sense of its universal form. The side-effect of the sense of 'universality' of deprivation is, however, the feeling of deprivation's incurability: whatever I do inside the realm of 'life politics', deprivation won't go away. It is bound to remain my non-negotiable destiny as long as my conceivable actions stay confined to the interior of that realm.

This circumstance, I believe, goes a long way towards explaining the 'back to tribes' phenomenon described in the previous chapter.

*

This departure is a combined side-effect of two parallel processes: of the globalization of powers (at least of the most potent among them, capable of determining our fate) and of information (at least the most influential in shaping out whatever we are presented with and pressed to absorb and accept as the truth, the whole truth and nothing but the truth); in short, of what can be called the 'widening of horizons' or even 'effacement of horizons (in the sense of the limits to vision)' – horizons of, simultaneously, interdependence and comparability. That widening of horizons is, by a common and apparently well-grounded consent, the accomplishment of the new technology of informatics, now approaching a fully and truly ecumenical – for everybody – accessibility.

The stretching of cognitive horizons to the extent of

the totality of the space within reach of video cameras and smart phones (and consequently of the World-Wide-Web) puts paid to the idea of 'neighbourhood' defined in terms of physical distance, distinguishing the accessibility and familiarity of 'proximity' from the unapproachability and obscurity of the 'far away'. Indeed, it casts out of use that metonymical logic (or 'sympathetic magic', as James George Fraser named it in his *Golden Bough*), in which the phenomenon and the concept of relative deprivation were both grounded.

The contents of the 'neighbourhood', in the sense of 'people within reach' – or George Herbert Mead's 'significant others' who form the 'me' forcefully engaged in the continuous dialogue/interaction with the 'I' – are not, as a consequence, inscribed as before in a continuous/contiguous space, but fragmented – diffuse and scattered; were the fragments marked on a geographical map, they would be akin to an archipelago of diasporas – an assemblage of islands separated and keeping distance between each other while linked by mental/cultural proximity sustained by and sustaining their shared identity (or, as in the case of 'significant others', by the meaning, relevance and importance assigned to them by the cartographer). In practice, this means that the 'reference group' deployed as a yardstick of suffered discrimination no longer needs to be coherently composed. In most cases, it is indeed heterogeneous, disjointed and all in all logically flawed and unsustainable. Nor does it need to aspire to durability, or legitimize itself by the presumption of constancy and staying power – the most common tendency being to compose and decompose such groups, ad hoc.

I suggest that this new existential status for the sense

of deprivation is an answer, or at least a significant part of an answer, to the question of whether the fast-rising degree of 'objective' inequality, however it is measured, will lead to the emergence of the 'revolutionary situation', as our ancestors would have supposed; and if it will not, then why not?

*

Nelson D. Schwartz gave the title 'In the Age of Privilege, Not Everyone is in the Same Boat' to his report, published in the 23 April 2016 issue of the *New York Times*,[18] of the new super-luxurious but also – significantly – secluded, sheltered, hidden and supremely private enclaves offered to the new minute, yet unstoppably self-enriching, class of the 'extremely wealthy' by travel companies, which, having discovered in the super rich a new uniquely profitable market, are shifting their attention and care to catering for their needs and whims: to the intensive, as distinct from the heretofore favoured extensive method of obtaining an, as swift as it is impressive, rise in the costs:effects ratio. The metaphor of 'the same boat' (implying its opposition to the alternative of an 'utterly different' boat) was prompted by Schwartz's combination of the two objects he selected for his in-depth research: Norwegian and 'North Caribbean' seafaring companies. The phenomena he found there are, however, cases of an immensely wider tendency, currently gaining unprecedented impetus.

Schwartz starts by quoting Emmanuel Saez, Professor of Economics at the University of California, Berkeley, to set the stage on which inequality is subjected to honing and grooming while being continually enriched by ever new dimensions added by the purveyors and caterers to the meaning of being counted in the top 1 per cent of the very rich, always greedy for more distinctions and privileges. Saez:

> estimates that the top 1 percent of American households now controls 42 percent of the nation's wealth, up from less than 30 percent two decades ago. The top 0.1 percent accounts for 22 percent, nearly double the 1995 proportion ... Today, ever greater resources are being invested in winning market share at the very top of the pyramid, sometimes at the cost of diminished service for the rest of the public. While middle-class incomes are stagnating, the period since the end of the Great Recession has been a boom time for the very rich and the businesses that cater to them.

As a joint effect of the market logic and the dedicated efforts of the market trendsetters eager to capitalize on their discovery of a new and exquisitely profitable market –

> from 2010 to 2014, the number of American households with at least $1 million in financial assets jumped by nearly one-third, to just under seven million, according to a study by the Boston Consulting Group. For the $1 million-plus cohort, estimated wealth grew by 7.2 percent annually from 2010 to 2014, eight times the pace of gains for families with less than $1 million

– the whole life of the most wealthy, not just its domestic parts, is lived in a sort of mobile 'gated community' – a bubble inside a tight, impermeable carapace, non-translucent and non-transparent to any of the inferior, 'less than $1 million', folks.

One is entitled to surmise that the two categories

spend their whole lives in two mutually incommunicado worlds, whose thick and sturdy walls those with 'over $1 million' never need to cross, and those with 'less than $1 million' are never allowed to cross. Thanks to the new accoutrements furnished and purveyed by the companies pandering to the self-alienating and self-enclosing predispositions of the very rich, the inhabitants of the two worlds may spend their lives never meeting each other – let alone sharing their modes of life, life experiences and the life philosophy all these gestate. For all practical intents and purposes, the occupants of the two (above $1 million and below $1 million) categories seem to develop and use mutually untranslatable languages. The widely noted divergence (indeed, the unbridgeable gap) between the languages of the elite and those of the rest of humankind has hardly ever, since the Middle Ages, been so profound as it is becoming at the start to the twenty-first century. In addition to the degree of comfort, the volume and potency of their capabilities and their life-style, the superior of the 'two nations' has acquired a language all of its own. By the same token, the bisection of society into two nations has now reached its completion.

There is one important proviso, though – also hinted on, even if only briefly, in Schwartz's report:

> As coach passengers pile into giant 747s and A380s, for example, 'a glimpse of a shower or private suite creates a marker in people's minds', said Alex Dichter, a director at McKinsey who works with major airlines. 'A lot of brands use products like these as an aspirational tool, and class segregation can create something to which people can aspire.'

The sublime and exotic charms of the world inhabited by those with 'over $1 million' have also an important function to perform – one that calls for somewhat compromising its non-transparency and invisibility to outsiders. To be properly performed, that function requires allowing those outsiders an occasional glimpse of the breath-taking and mind-boggling wonders enjoyed daily by the 'over $1 million' but refused – and, thus far, off limits – to the rest. Consumer markets are set to efface the 'relative' part of the 'relative deprivation' – an undertaking rightly believed to spur its victims into more redemptive, compensatory action. As I tried to argue in my book *Does the Richness of the Few Benefit Us All?*,[19] the 'trickle-down effect' of wealth on popular well-being is, by and large, a myth; but I need to add that such an effect on the popular sense of deprivation and consequently level of aspiration is stern reality.

The cases of hermetic enclosure and of (even if rare and partial) openness are both valid, each in its own way, while remaining at cross-purposes. To set in motion their aspiration-raising (and so also, hopefully, their market-widening) potential, the delights reserved for the fabulously rich are on display on myriads of the mass-media monitors hand-held in slums of Mumbai as much as in the apartments in 'gated communities', but, just like the other messages-on-screen, they risk being taken for the products of the script-writer's imagination, even when equipped with an assurance of being 'based on true events'. A 'glimpse of a shower or private suite' on the way to a cramped seat in the overcrowded 'tourist' section of the jumbo jet turns for that reason into a crucially important act of authenticating endorsement: well, after all, my suspicions notwithstanding,

what they showed in that movie was not a fairy tale or
a figment of fanciful imagination – it was real, and so
it was worth taking seriously and deserved/justified the
ensuing effort. Only if this effect is achieved, will the
crossbar for the leap of aspiration be likely to be raised
as intended.

*

Daniel Raventós – and a rapidly rising number of his
comrades-in-arms – considers 'basic income' to be the
cornerstone of any future House of Equality. 'Basic
income', he says,[20] is 'an income paid by the state to
each full member or accredited resident of a society,
regardless of whether he or she wishes to engage in paid
employment, or is rich or poor or, in other words, inde-
pendently of any other sources of income that person
might have, and irrespective of cohabitation arrangements in the domestic sphere'.

Agreeing on this point with the postulates of the
Earth Network of Basic Income, Raventós insists
that, to make sure that, once made into a law, basic
income does social good and avoids doing evil, it must
be guided by the following three principles: it must
be paid (1) to individuals rather than households, (2)
irrespective of any income from other sources, and (3)
without requiring the performance of any work or the
willingness to accept a job if offered (p. 9). Let me
observe that those three principles set the idea of basic
income apart from the explicit or tacit presumptions of
the contemporary practices of whatever remains of the
original philosophy of the 'welfare state' – their focusing on households instead of individuals, their tendency
to make the entitlements to social provisions 'means-

tested', and the current trend of replacing 'welfare' with 'workfare'.

The Earth Network of Basic Income, as well as Daniel Raventós himself, looks over the heads of the current designers and managers of social welfare provisions back to the roots of the welfare-state's history: William Beveridge's report on *Social Insurance and Allied Services* was met with almost unanimous approval from the general public and leading opinion-making institutions in Britain at the time of its publication in 1942 (one of the few voices of opposition was that of Kingsley Wood, then the Chancellor of the Exchequer in the Tory–Labour coalition goverment, insisting on the impracticality of the financial commitments the Beveridge Report implied). The intention to revive and restore the assumptions on which the Beveridge Report rested (the premises later gradually, yet consistently, abandoned and all but forgotten by the succession of Tory and Labour governments) shows through the subtitle of Raventós' study/manifesto. William (later Lord) Beveridge was neither a conservative nor a socialist; he considered himself a liberal – having acquired the right to do so by faithfully following the essential precepts of liberal ideology to their logically ultimate fulfilment. Individual freedom being cast by that ideology as the supreme value and the cardinal commandment, as well as the preeminent objective (indeed, a meta-objective) of political practice, that value could be properly served only if the 'material conditions of freedom' were met. They haven't been met, however (as much then as now, again), for a large part of British society – a part smarting as it was (and in quite a few respects continues to be, or has reasons to fear becoming) under the burden of the five 'giant evils' in society: squalor, ignorance, want, idleness and disease. Until those giant evils are confronted point blank and forced to retreat, 'freedom' will remain for that large part of British society an empty slogan, and for all practical intents an illusion adding a scorching insult to the already hurtfully inflamed injury. This declared aim of liberals – to satisfy all the material conditions of freedom – is today no less distant than it was when William Beveridge sat down to compose his report – or, perhaps, it is even more distant than then?

Admitting that the 'basic income idea' was seen (certainly on the left of the political spectrum) as 'a way to alleviate inequality', Paul Mason[21] adds a new powerful argument justifying its urgency: basic income 'is a solution to a much bigger problem: the disappearance of work itself'. What he says, roughly, is that, until quite recently, both the Panglosses and the Cassandras of this world lived jointly in what André Gorz dubbed the 'utopia based on work' – but that the blow, striking equally all sectors of the political spectrum, similarly caught unprepared, is that the ground on which that utopia was stood has been pulled from under its foundations – by, among many other revelations, the 2013 Oxford Martin School's finding that 'in the next two decades 47% of US jobs would be in danger of being lost to automation', or the McKinsey Global Institute's conclusion that '140 million knowledge workers are at risk of the same fate', as well as by our new awareness that, if the past tides of 'deskilling and job destruction went alongside the creation of new, high value jobs and a higher-wage consumption culture', automation 'reduces the need for work in one sector without necessarily creating it in another'.

*

All the same, the prospects of public pressure forcing the 'basic income' to turn fairly soon from a noble yet utopian, 'Land of Cockaigne'-style idea into a rough-and-ready reality are, to say the least, bleak and discouraging – particularly when it comes to the third of the conditions spelled out by Raventós: abolishment of the means tests *together* with the cutting off of the right to basic income for people engaged in remunerated employment. Around these two interconnected postulates the resistance to the implementation of the 'basic income' project is arguably the strongest – even if (or rather because) it rests mostly on incomprehension and confusion of values. If anything, successive gains on the road to implementation of the 'basic income' agenda are proving to be but temporary and, under pressure, tend to be withdrawn one by one, as are the principles of the state-administered social services laid at the foundation of the welfare state.

The official summary of the symposium held on 11 March 2009 by the Joseph Rowntree Foundation, in cooperation with the School of Politics of the University of York (a symposium dedicated to the discussion of Philippe van Parijs' fundamental contribution to the basic income project), starts with the following diagnosis of the present-day stage of the welfare state's convoluted and controversial history:

Over the past three decades British Governments have moved away from the philosophy of universalism, which once underpinned the welfare state. Targeting and selection are fast becoming a norm while benefits and services are becoming the exception. The welfare-reform bill currently going through parliament – which, among other things, insists that mentally ill people and single parents with children as young as three must be available for work before becoming eligible for benefits – is indicative of this trend.

This trend, the summary points out, is not confined to Britain; the US Congress passed in 1996 the 'Personal Responsibility and Work Opportunity Reconciliation Act' that 'narrowed the eligibility criteria to the very needy, limited the receipt of benefits to five years, and insisted that all recipients undertake work or work training'.

There is a watershed kind of difference between the 'philosophy of universalism' – basic income as an inalienable citizen's right and endorsement of the duty of the community to each and any of its members – and the focus on the 'most needy' and 'where it hurts most'. The first is the natural accompaniment to the era of recognition and promotion of 'human rights'; the second drives society back to the times of Victorian poorhouses and workhouses, their natural home. In that home, there was no room to accommodate either the concept of endemic, ingrained human dignity or the right to 'pursue happiness', which the American Declaration of Independence proclaimed. Poor- and workhouses set their aims at a much lower level: that of the biological survival of wards (a high death rate was a side-effect, not the explicit and deliberate premise, of lowering that level). So set, the aim had to be twofold: to postpone the inmates' death, and to prevent them from joining in life of the other, non-stigmatized, 'normal' (because they looked after themselves and so hoped to stay 'self-sufficient') humans. Being admitted to a poorhouse or workhouse came in a package deal of stigma: blame and shame of someone below the threshold of fully fledged humanity. In a world that takes work and soldiery for the norm of life, and working and soldiering for the certificate of social membership and social position, people with no work, and so with no self-secured means of survival, could not but be branded as outcasts. Demanding cancellation of means tests and independence of the right to social standing from the presence or absence of remunerated employment, breaks radically with the languishing legacy of the mindset generative of poorhouses and workhouses, which the old/new schemes of means tests and workfare are set to resurrect and return to grace.

More and more researchers are gathering empirical proofs that giving people money with no strings attached – a strategy that prompts them to self-assert while simultaneously rendering self-assertion possible and putting it in their reach – is, in opposition to what its no less numerous critics aver, also 'good business' from the point of view of governments' budgets and the nation's wealth: it is an asset rather than a liability, adding to instead of detracting from the levels of the nation's wealth and income. One of these researchers, and probably the one casting his net most widely (much too widely for me to be able to present here his enormous catch), is the already-quoted Rutger Bregman, who even cites *The Economist*, not known to be a tribune for universal basic income (UBI) enthusiasts, to document the emerging consent on the matter: the 'most efficient way to spend money on the homeless might be to give it to them'.[22]

Bregman calls us to fundamentally rethink the legacy

of the 'welfare state' mindset, shaped up as it was in the times of the 'society of work', but out of place in the present times which that work, inadvertently, managed to mould and put in place: 'The welfare state, which should foster people's sense of security and pride, has degenerated into a system of suspicion and shame' (p. 69). What I would add is that, instead of redistributing wealth, that arrangement still called, by inertia, the 'welfare state' is by now in charge of branding the condition of 'being on welfare' with a social stigma, thereby acquitting the public conscience of all guilt it bears for the part it plays in tolerating (and exacerbating) the social inequality that ought to have been a heartrending call to arms. 'Being on welfare', read commonly as meaning 'being a sponger' or 'claiming' (and getting) 'something for nothing', is recycled by such a deformed and degenerated welfare-state mindset into a badge of shame, as well as the proof one needs (*all* the proof in fact) of the less than full entitlement of 'people on welfare' to human rights, of the corruption and depravity of their characters, and, all in all, of social redundancy.

Unlike (indeed, in stark opposition to) the philosophy behind the present-day version of the 'welfare state', the philosophy underpinning the 'basic income' augurs and promotes inclusion, instead of exclusion, as well as social solidarity and social integration instead of fissiparousness of bonds of solidarity, and social divisiveness.

These considerations justify the viewing of basic income as a tremendous social and moral gain that no other prescription for dealing with inequality seems be able to procure. But the gains are promised to be, in fact, even more manifold. Calling on us to 'talk different, think different', Bregman quotes for instance,

from *Just Give Money to the Poor*, a book composed
by a University of Manchester team of scholars lead by
Armando Barrientos and David Hulme and published
in 2001,[23] reporting that the benefits of programmes of
the basic-income kind have been found to include also
the following: '(1) Households put the money to good
use, (2) poverty declines', 'diverse long-term benefits for
income, health, and tax revenues, and (3) the programs
cost less than the alternatives' (p. 59). Or, to give one
more example, this time referring to the findings drawn
from her 2003 research by Jane Costello,[24] a Duke
University professor, who, having asked 'what, then, is
the cause of mental health problems among the poor?
Nature or culture?', concluded that both are, 'because
the stress of poverty puts people genetically predisposed
to develop an illness or disorder at an elevated risk.
But there's a more important takeaway from this study.
Genes can't be undone. Poverty can' (p. 99).

'The main argument for UBI', writes Philippe van
Parijs, 'is founded on the view of justice.'[25] 'Justice' he
defines as tantamount to creating institutions 'designed
to best secure *real freedom* to all'. Note: it is not just
the right to be free that is at stake, but freedom's *reality* (what John Rawls called 'worth of freedom' – while
Isaiah Berlin dubbed it – alas, in his misled intention,
dismissively – 'positive freedom', in order to set it apart
from the 'negative freedom', freedom from constraints,
that he advocated instead). For the UBI advocates, as
much as for their predecessors, the designers of the welfare state, that 'positive freedom' – i.e., the capability to
self-assert and to follow ones' choices – is, however, an
indispensable concomitant of the 'negative' one, once
it is recast as the warrant against rendering the latter a

recipe for the destitution of a large number of society's members. Freedom is worthy when it and the human potential it is assumed to throw wide open are real; for a great number of humans, it will, however, stop far short of reality unless it is accompanied by UBI or some sort of functional equivalent of it. 'The worth or real value of a person's liberty', as van Parijs insists, 'depends on the resources the person has at her command to make use of her liberty', while, for the whole operation to serve the cause of social justice, 'the distribution of opportunity – understood as access to the means that people need for doing what they might want to do – [needs to] be designed to offer the greatest possible real opportunity to those with fewest opportunities'.

In addition to containing a neat and concise re-statement of van Parijs' position, the quoted book is a collection of critical assessments of various items in his programme, which between themselves provide a near-complete survey of the relatively brief, yet stormy, history of the idea and its present condition – as well as an insight into its possible chances, and obstacles on the road to exploiting them properly. Among these assessments, Claus Offe's entry stands out for its comprehensiveness and its – on the whole successful – venture to reach the roots of both its rising popularity and the odds averse to putting it into operation.

What Offe undertakes is nothing less than prodding Parijs' theory to offer, as every good theory should be able to, 'a theory about itself'; 'The theorist must answer, among others, the question: why do so many people oppose my theory?'[26] This is a serious – perhaps the most serious – question yearning for an answer, considering that: 'while interest in and openness toward

UBI schemes are generally on the rise, and not only so in the advanced economies, nobody would seriously claim that the reality of Basic Income ... is just around the corner anywhere. Why not?' (p. 112).

In the inventory of initial answers, the most usual of suspects, the fear caused by the anticipation of freedom (which, although 'passionate and exaggerated, need not be outright paranoiac') comes naturally at the top of the roll call. But 'who has which reasons to fear what from the freedom that would follow on UBI?' Not surprisingly, it is employers who open the list, having a double reason to do so: first, fearing that 'their control over workers will be weakened, as workers would have a liveable withdrawal option'; and second, suspecting that a UBI will require a rate of ... taxation that in turn will involve a downward compression of the scale of net income' (p. 113).

These and other fears aroused in different quarters need to be taken seriously – as Offe rightly warns and duly requires. He also suggests ways to put some at least of those fears to rest, or at any rate to mitigate them and render them somewhat easier to outbalance, outweigh and overcome. The most principal among them, and most innovative, are '*gradualism* and *reversibility*. The idea is to provide a context in which people can change their preferences through learning, as in the saying that appetite comes with the eating (rather than with coercive feeding)' (p. 114). Perhaps the most interesting – because arguably the most promising – among them is what Offe calls the 'sabbatical account' '(of, say, ten years) to which every adult person is entitled and upon which she can draw at any time ... in the form of chunks of time of at least six months, and use the free time, which is covered by the flat-rate income, for whatever purpose she chooses'. He predicts that the most desirable, while at the same time highly probable, effect of this way of reinforcing the truly and fully universal foundations of freedom will rebound in its impact 'upon what we used to call "work humanization" and the gradual elimination of particularly "bad" jobs' (p. 117).

One of the most serious obstacles (even if of a technical/administrative, rather than 'antagonistic class interests', kind) piled up on the way to the otherwise pragmatically sensible 'road map' to UBI sketched by Offe is, however, the likelihood that a practical attempt at its implementation will fairly quickly confirm the suspicion that the introduction of the UBI regime can only be conducted either universally or not at all. Offe is clear about this – perhaps in the last account fundamental – snag: at least on EU territory, UBI 'cannot be introduced in one country alone'. It cannot, we should specify, as long as the network of political institutions dedicated to servicing the EU territory in its totality is, for most practical intents and purposes, absent or politically fragmented – a circumstance in one sense specific to the EU, but in another sense a manifestation of the world-wide institutional separation of the ability to get things done from the capability of deciding which things need and ought to be done.

These considerations do not, however, have to be taken for an argument against entrenching the UBI regime in human practice; on the contrary, they may and should be used to capitalize on the likely rise in the attractiveness and popularity of UBI for the sake of re-marrying power and politics now in divorce: for instance, though still on a much grander scale, for the 'implementation of a "social" Europe that might be capable of providing some much-needed meaning and broad popular appeal to the project of European integration' (p. 118).

I suggest that it would be a grave error to argue that the UBI project is doomed because the well-documented facts of the day point to a prevailing, perhaps even overwhelming, 'back to inequality' trend. That argument needs, and can, be reversed: the vitality of the UBI project, as one of the few essential ingredients of the contemporary 'utopia for the realists', can be utilized as a uniquely powerful weapon in the struggle to reverse that gruesome and dangerous, potentially catastrophic, trend.

4
Back to the Womb

'Back to the self' has been born as a battle-cry of the war
of liberation from the horrors of tribal imprisonment,
resurrected by the still-birth of its ostensible cosmopolitan alternative – just as 'back to tribes' was, and
still remains, the motto of running-for-shelter from the
abominations of the loneliness of the orphaned/bereaved
individuals of the post-liberation era. Both calls are poisons, curiously serving as antidotes to each other.

In the 'Privatisation of Hope: Capitalism vs.
Solidarity, Yesterday and Today'[1] – a succinct, yet all
the same trenchant and incisive, and first and foremost
sincere (one is tempted to say: audaciously sincere), vivisection of human bonds – currently falling apart as a
consequence of having been by and large abandoned
to individual humans' own wits, their chronically inadequate resources, and the self-referential nature of their
concerns, initiatives and undertakings – published in
the *Boston Review* on 26 April 2016, Ronald Aronson
asserts:

Hope is being privatized. Throughout the world, but especially in the United States and the United Kingdom, a seismic shift is underway, displacing aspirations and responsibilities from the larger society to our own individual universes. The detaching of personal expectations from the wider world transforms both . . .

We have not lost all hope over the past generation; there is a maddening profusion of personal hopes. Under attack has been the kind of hope that is social, the motivation behind movements to make the world freer, more equal, more democratic, and more livable.

In a nutshell:

At one time, workers understood that they could improve their conditions by collectively asserting themselves; now workers understand that their best option is to protect themselves *by themselves*. Among self-seekers, experiences of class and solidarity are impossible and irrelevant. As [Steve] Fraser says, when the self is the only viable site of betterment, when there is no possible gain from collective action, collective consciousness seems 'foolish, naive, woolly-headed or, on the contrary, sinful and seditious'.

Once abandoned to the market game, which they had little choice but to join in the double capacity of sellers and the commodity on sale, commodified humans are pushed and/or cajoled to perceive their being-in-the-world as an aggregation and succession of buying–selling transactions, and to regard the population of that world as an accumulation of so many other peddlers flaunting and haggling the wares each one of them displays on a privately owned and run market stall.

The people you meet on first entering that world, and

then again and again upon successive entries to each one of its compartments, are most likely to 'interpellate'[2] you, and equally likely to be interpellated by you, as rivals and competitors – from time to time, maybe, as candidates for an occasional ad-hoc alliance, but hardly ever as natural brothers-/sisters-in-arms – whether actual or destined to become so. We are currently being forcefully pushed – though without much resistance on our part being evoked – back, to the early nineteenth century, when the peasants in many countries of Europe, and craftsmen and artisans in all of them, were expropriated on an accelerating pace of their means of production, and thereby also of their social standing and social capital. Since then, they have been crowded into the space of a 'life nasty, brutish and short' because it was conducted in a world engaged in the 'war of all against all' – a world populated by the miserable like them, like them faceless and not fully human, and like them finding their new surroundings to be as alienating as they are hostile. It took them many decades to discover a common interest in that anonymous crowd clocking in and out of the early capitalist factories and to crown that discovery with the notion of 'solidarity' that ushered them into the era of experiments, aborted or stillborn attempts, false starts, defeats and short-term triumphs stored in long-term memory; and still more time to invent, institutionalize and practise a systemic and systematic solidary action aimed at replacing enslavement with emancipation.

We are now in an era similar in its ambience. Some of us derive endurance from hoping for the forthcoming of new, more promising beginnings for all. Some others, disenchanted and exasperated by hopes addicted to frustration, invest their aspirations in turning back to the past. But it seems that a large majority among us don't care one way or the other (either about the future or about the past), busying themselves instead in finding ways to disarm the unendurable prospects with gadgets likely to deliver small – but day in, day out – satisfactions: cutting down on ambitions and expectations, having first retreated into the deceptively safe shelter of self-concern and self-reference. We haven't yet started, however, earnestly to take note of (let alone to draw conclusions from) the deceitfulness of that shelter's safety and the disingenuity of self-reference. Blowing on singed fingers, most of us go on believing that – as Fraser noted – collective consciousness (not to mention collective action) is either seditious or naive.

Frustration and the pain of singed fingures are almost genuine – but conclusions most people draw from them in practice, even if not always in theory, are not the only conceivable or even the sole convincing, let alone 'foregone' or pre-determined; on the contrary, they are perched on several layers of tacit make-believe presumptions, none of which holds much water. Jim Jackson, Professor of Sustainable Development at the University of Surrey, managed to embrace all of these levels in a single concise phrase: 'It's a story about us, people, *being persuaded to spend money we don't have on things we don't need to create impressions that won't last on people we don't care about.*'[3] Cut to the dry bones, this phrase means: we have been drawn into all those senseless preoccupations and routines, which we came to trust as the *foolproof* recipe for confirming our *illusory* status.

To apply Robert Merton's memorable distinction

between the manifest and latent functions of social arrangements and the behavioural patterns they insinuate and demand, the manifest function of the mode of life imposed by the consumerist culture is to service clients' needs and choices and facilitate their gratification, while the latent function (as Merton suggests, the factual engine of the whole arrangement) is to allow users to reconcile with and adjust to a life in which the chronic lack of servicing of genuine needs is made liveable by the stratagem of illusory gratification of the phantom ones.

Drawing on presently all-too-common – and therefore familiar – manifestations of that rule in operation, Umberto Eco offers (in one of his 1991 essays[4]) an outstandingly, uniquely perceptive autopsy of its mechanism:

> The man with power is the man who is not required to answer every call; on the contrary, he is always – as the saying goes – in a meeting . . .
>
> So anyone who flaunts a portable phone as a symbol of power is, on the contrary, announcing to all and sundry his desperate, subaltern position, in which he is obliged to snap to attention, even when making love, if the CEO happens to telephone . . . The fact that he uses, ostentatiously, his cellular phone is proof that he doesn't know these things, and it is the confirmation of his social banishment, beyond appeal.

Steve Fraser's eye-opening study, researched meticulously and in-depth, of what he calls *The Age of Acquiescence*[5] – a genuine compendium of factors joining forces in the job of bolstering such 'men with power' inside the castles to which they retreat, and of making them immune to the acts of dissent and protest by those barred access – is subtitled *The Life and Death of American Resistance to Organized Wealth and Power.* His question is not why *did* 'Occupy Wall Street' happen (a question with an answer too obvious to demand a 500–pages-long study), but why it *didn't* 'happen much sooner than it did'. And, as we may add with the benefit of hindsight when reading that book two years after it left the printing presses, why did it fade, wilt and grind to a halt so soon, leaving little if any trace on Wall Street's practices and eroding next to nothing of insurance of the 'men in power' against the thoughts and deeds of the remaining 99 per cent of the nation? Particularly if 'the political class prescribed what people already had enough of: yet another dose of austerity, plus a faith-based belief in a "recovery" that for the 99% of Americans would never be much more than an optical illusion', and that in those years 'the hopes of ordinary people for a chance at a decent future waned and bitterness set in'?

*

Somewhere on the road from the early-modern, positive, boisterous, assertive and self-confident utopia to the present-day diffident, dejected and defeatist retrotopia, Pygmalion, remembered (thanks to Ovid's *Metamorphoses*) for having fallen in love with the charms of Galatée, the ivory sculpture of his own creation, met Narcissus, who had fallen in love with his own beauty – but, in the last account, with the impressions it made on surfaces capable of reflecting it (though not necessarily, as in the case of river waters, of retaining them).

In his epoch-making study of contemporary narcissism,[6] Christopher Lasch announces the forthcoming
substitution of the 'psychological man', the ultimate
product of bourgeois individualism, for the 'economic
man', the orthodox typical personality of the capitalist
society. The psychological man, the typical personality honed and groomed by the capitalist society in its
present-day consumerist/narcissist stage, is, in sharp
contrast to his now displaced predecessor:

> haunted not by guilt but by anxiety. He seeks not to inflict
> his own certainties on others but to find a meaning in life
> . . . He forfeits the security of group loyalties and regards
> everyone as a rival for the favours conferred by the pater-
> nalistic state . . . Fiercely competitive in his demand for
> approval and acclaim, he distrusts competition because
> he associates it unconsciously with an unbridled urge to
> destroy... Acquisitive in the sense that his cravings have no
> limits . . . [he] demands immediate gratification and lives in
> a state of restless perpetually unsatisfied desire . . . To live
> for a moment is the prevailing passion – to live for yourself,
> not for your predecessors or posterity. (pp. 22–3, 30)

Lasch concludes that the resemblance of 'the contemporary narcissist, in his self-absorption and illusion of
grandeur, to the "imperial self" so often celebrated in
nineteenth-century American literature' is but superfi-
cial (p. 35) – and let me add: just like the resemblance
between Pygmalion/producer and Narcissus/consumer.
Let me also comment, however, right away, that this
resemblance cannot be dismissed as accidental or contingent. After all, going back to the narcissist model
of self in an attempt to incarnate the 'imperial self' of
yore was exactly the promise of the society filling count-

less shop-shelves with self-identification kits, complete with instructions for their assembly: a cause-and-effect succession with the resulting situation not at all 'superficially' similar to the plight of all other aspects of the 'back to the past' phenomenon – of which the 'back to the self' case is but one.

One of a few fundamental questions is whether the narcissist tendencies need to be viewed and treated (and, of course, drawn into the orbit of medical charge) as '*personality* disorders', as they are commonly cast, presented and debated, or as a '*society* disorder'. Are they multiplied, yet still marginal (and bound/hoped to stay marginal), individual abnormalities – or the symptoms of emergent normality? Is this a manifestation of resetting the options offered by a changing human condition – or of new proclivities of characters now saddled with the obligation and task between them? In short, is it a matter of sociology – or psychology? These are difficult questions, searching in vain for unambiguous answers if the ecotype in which the narcissist phenomenon has been conceived and begotten is taken under the microscope; a socioscape correctly observed, recorded and painted by Anthony Elliott:

> We live today in a world in which people struggle with changes in sexual mores, battle against the unsettling of relationships, experiment with different definitions of self and search for meaning in negotiating the interpersonal demands of everyday life. Such engagements with the broader canvas of culture in terms of its meaning for the inner life entails the recognition of choice. Choice, in this context, means understanding the active, creative ways in which a sense of self is shaped and reshaped, while at the

same time acknowledging the profound influence of other people and of culture upon our thinking about the private sphere.[7]

Lasch's firm, and extensively as well as intensely argued, opinion is that 'experiences of inner emptiness, loneliness and inauthenticity', by which the narcissist response is triggered, 'arise from the warlike conditions that pervade American society, from the dangers and uncertainty that surround us, and from loss of confidence in the future' (p. 64). This hypothesis strikes one as true, nothing but true – though not, however, as the whole truth. What is missing is the link between the experience of an unmanageable mass of risks and the permanent anxiety that mass generates – along with the narcissist syndrome. That link, I suggest, is brought into being by a wholesale shift of responsibility for life's failures onto the shoulders of life's actors.

When asked by the nymph Liriope, Narcissus' mother, to forecast her son's fate, the soothsayer Tiresias in Book 3 of Ovid's *Metamorphoses*, seeing it all because of his blindness, predicted a long life, on condition that Narcissus 'never recognizes himself'. As it happens, the contemporary Narcissi are forced by the culture into which they are born to do little else but try as hard as they can to 'recognize themselves': each one, himself or herself. In fact, this is the main cause of their turning into Narcissi – starting from the tender years of what will be a life-long nurture, training and drill.

Sigmund Freud[8] was cautious, circumspect and prudent regarding the human condition and psyche – avoiding unambiguous commitment when it came to deciding whether that urge to 'recognize oneself' despite

the warnings is a symptom of a disorder, or the ubiquitous proclivity of the human psyche. To expose the
intrinsic difficulty of a straightforward and definite resolution of that dilemma, Freud expanded the extant
clinical description of narcissism (in the 1899 Paul
Näcke version, then recognized as authoritative, the
'attitude of a person who treats his own body in the
same way in which the body of a sexual object is ordi-
narily treated') so that the notion might 'claim a place
in the regular course of human sexual development . . .
Narcissism in this sense would not be a perversion, but
the libidinal complement to the egoism of the instinct
of preservation (that may justifiably be attributed to
every living creature)' (pp. 3–4). In his own extended
version, 'narcissism' stands for 'two fundamental characteristics: megalomania and diversion of interest from
the external world – from people and things' (p. 4). The
two named characteristics are nevertheless intimately
connected: 'The libido that has been withdrawn from
the external world has been directed to the ego' (p. 5).
There is, so to speak, a synthetic/antithetic *Haßliebe*
interaction between the two: 'We see also, broadly
speaking, an antithesis between ego-libido and object-
libido. The more of the one is employed, the more the
other becomes depleted' (p. 7). In Freud's approach,
'narcissism' could still be seen as a perversion of the
natural human predisposition, though not an affliction
setting the afflicted out as 'clinical cases'. Freud refuses
to conclude 'that human beings are divided into two
sharply differentiated groups . . . We assume rather that
both kinds of object-choice [anaclitic *and* narcissistic]
are open to each individual, though he may show pref-
erence for one or the other.' The 'primary narcissism

in anyone may however manifest itself in a dominant fashion' (pp. 23–4). I suggest that this possibility anticipated by Freud in 1914 has turned by 2014 into a norm regulating our behaviour.

*

The effects of Freud's premonition turning into a psychosocial norm have been recorded thus by Rutger Bregman: 'What's important now', is 'to just be yourself' and 'do your thing'. So freedom, our ostensibly highest ideal, 'has become empty'.[9] What we lack most painfully is 'a reason to get out of bed in the morning'. No wonder that 'never before have so many young adults been seeing psychiatrists'; nor have there been so many early-career burnouts or so many antidepressant pills swallowed; though he also finds a silver lining in this particular cloud: 'The widespread nostalgia, the yearning for a past that never really was, suggests that we still have ideals, even if we have buried them alive.'[10]

Having lost (or turned our backs on) all visions of an alternative – better – society of the future – associating the future, if not with 'worse than the present' then with 'more of the same' (another increment in salary, another career promotion, another new gadget, another holiday, another shift in fashion of dress, cars, wallpapers) – no wonder that, when seeking genuinely meaningful ideas, we turn, nostalgically, to the buried (prematurely?) grand ideas of the past. We are allowed to conclude that the vision of a 'better life' has disentangled itself from its made-in-Heaven marriage to the future. On the way to their divorce, it has also been commodified, relegated to the charge of consumer markets, and abominably impoverished by having been emptied of its ethical relevance.

But what about the very idea of 'better' and 'improvement'? Are the meanings we are prompted and inclined to conceive and imbue into those all-but-immortal springs of our efforts immune to the on-going cultural revolution? As Cederström and André Spicer have found in their study,[11] a new meaning – that of 'wellness' – tends now to displace and elbow out those remembered from the still relatively recent past. The 'wellness' itself 'has become a moral demand . . . As consumers, we are required to curate a lifestyle aimed at maximizing our wellbeing' (that is, let me explain, our – personal – health and fitness). Significantly, 'when health becomes an ideology, the failure to conform becomes a stigma'. People who 'fail to look after their bodies . . . are demonized as lazy, feeble or weak willed', 'as obscene deviants, unlawfully and unashamedly enjoying what every sensible person should resist' (pp. 3–4). The authors quote Steven Poole[12] on the matter of food becoming our present-day ideology, and on switching our trust when seeking answers to what we are prodded, by everyone from politicians and priests (in whom we have lost faith) to celebrity chefs and nutritionists, to consider as 'the big (existential) questions'. The shift is fully and truly seminal: when we *outsource* our intimate life and the search for a meaning to experts, 'coaching leads to the *insourcing* of responsibility' (italics added); 'We now have to blame ourselves for all conceivable problems' (p. 13).

Let me observe that, in as far as the acts of assuming responsibility and remaining faithful to it once it had been assumed form between themselves the heart of a moral attitude, the new 'back to the self' morality is grounded in redirecting responsibility (at any rate its prime component deserving most of our attention and concern) from 'out there' (i.e. from the Other, the near and dear, 'us', community, society, humanity, the Planet we share) towards *my* body: its dexterity, its capacity to deliver the gratification of 'wellness'. The collateral damage perpetrated by the shift in question is privatization and the self-referential essence of moral duty. The new morality has turned from centrifugal into centripetal: once the prime adhesive serving the process of interpersonal gap-bridging, distance-shortening and integration, it is joining now the large and still-swelling toolbox of division, separation, dissociation, alienation and laceration.

*

Regarding the current popular interest in the works of the novel-writer and philosopher Ayn Rand (1905–82), denigrated – if not downright dismissed and ignored – by both mainstream academic philosophy and authoritative literary criticism, Wikipedia supplies the following information:

> In 1991, a survey conducted for the Library of Congress and the Book-of-the-Month Club asked club members what the most influential book in the respondent's life was. Rand's *Atlas Shrugged* was the second most popular choice, after the Bible. Rand's books continue to be widely sold and read, with over 29 million copies sold as of 2013 (with about 10% of that total purchased for free distribution to schools by the Ayn Rand Institute). In 1998, Modern Library readers voted *Atlas Shrugged*

the 20th century's finest work of fiction, followed by *The Fountainhead* in second place, *Anthem* in seventh, and *We the Living* eighth.[13]

Of *Atlas Shrugged*, held by popular opinion (as recorded and documented by the sales figures) to be her *chef d'oeuvre*, Wikipedia opines that, despite receiving many negative reviews, it became an international bestseller. By and large, that estimate encapsulates the fate of all the rest of Rand's novels and philosophical essays. The story of Ayn Rand is a vivid testimony to the astonishingly wide, and all but insatiable, popular grassroots demand for the ideas that her writings promote. She must have spotted and put under cultivation a plot in the *Lebenswelt* of our contemporaries that had been overlooked and left barren by the elites of philosophy and literature – or, rather, a plot which those elites failed to give proper recognition to or refused to visit, let alone earnestly scrutinize. This bizarre and rather uncommon dissonance and divergence hints at the complexity, indeed inborn ambiguity, of the resurrection of Narcissus, and moreover at the status of the whole 'back to the self' movement in contemporary culture (for that very reason, the continued ignoring of the 'Ayn Rand phenomenon' by philosophers – and, for that matter, sociologists – seems to be nothing short of a grave error of judgement).

The plot in question was labelled by Rand 'objectivist ethics' (unpacked as 'an objective necessity of man's survival'), and the crop she aims to gather from its cultivation she labelled 'rational selfishness' (unpacked as 'values required for man's survival').[14] Note that the entity called 'human society' plays no role in that definitional ground-laying.

Rand is quite straightforward about the motives behind her choice of terms. Having confessed that, 'once in a while', she hears the question 'Why do you use the word "selfishness" to denote virtuous qualities of character, when that word antagonizes so many people to whom it does not mean the things you mean?', she admits that she answers that she does it 'for the reason that makes you afraid of it' (p. vii). She explains: 'Altruism [wrongly] declares that any action taken for the benefit of others is good, and any action taken for one's own benefit is evil' (p. viii). Such a declaration, endemically hostile to her vision of 'objective ethics', as she insists throughout, bears responsibility for 'insoluble conflicts and contradictions that have characterized human relationships and human societies throughout history'.

In the nutshell: Rand is after nothing less than a most radical re-valuation of values: after swapping the places assigned in the human condition and in the fundamental dilemma of human existence to – respectively – good and evil. She implies that the 'objective truth' stays with the Hobbesian description of human cohabitation as a war of all against all – while with the Leviathan, in which Hobbes invested the hope of peace, stays the guilt of belying that truth (and of all the awesome consequences of that lie). She also avers that the fact that ethics requires man's selfishness is meant to be perceived by many of us, repentant or unrepentant sinners that we are, as good tidings: a wholesale absolution for egoism, and acquittal from guilt, shame or sin wrongly ascribed to it by the perverse modern philosophizing. By even more of us – those who would wish, but don't dare, to sin – it could be welcomed as an a priori acquired indulgence for all future sins. However, it would also sound as a clarion call to caution, addressed to all of us, indiscriminately: a caution that 'stands to reason', because it is dictated by the very wholesale nature of the absolution and indulgence that 'objective ethics' has offered. Between themselves, the good and the bad news brought by 'objective ethics' are likely to render 'rational selfishness' nothing but a self-fulfilling hypothesis.

Not only are they likely to do this; we are witnessing them already doing so and progressing in the work done at a quite lively pace. And, as should have been expected because of the incurable duality of the message (simultaneously auguring and portending, promising and warning, emboldening and discouraging), a floodgate has already been opened wide to a rising tide of teach-yourself, do-it-yourself and how-to kinds of publications, all eager to draw their readers into the ranks of paying – instead of being paid – hands hired for the task.

The tide though is descending into two separated (not always neatly) riverbeds: one aimed at people looking for instructions on how to become a narcissist and enjoy it without a guilty conscience, and another for those wishing to know how to defend themselves from the narcissist preoccupations and dealings of others and to make them regret their thoughts and deeds. Another stream, originating perhaps from the same source, also splits into two rivulets: one directed at craving for a stretch of creativity-pregnant solitude, the other at sufferers from the pains of loneliness. What follows is but a few off-the-cuff samples drawn from the prolific flotsam and jetsam.

In the consoling words of Wilson Cooper, 'Loneliness is as common in human beings as the seashells on a beach.'[15] Fortunately, loneliness 'is only a feeling. And, if feelings can impact you greatly, this is one that can be transformed' (p. 13). How can this be done? Remember: 'No one can love you until you can love yourself ... You cannot expect feelings from someone else to replace what you do not think of yourself. If you already have issues with self acceptance, no amount of praise from others will ever get rid of that' (p. 15). It does not matter much what others around you value or censure in your self. And so, 'learn to be brave' (p. 19). Don't be ashamed of betraying your loneliness in public: 'There could be a new restaurant that you want to check out, or even a concert that you've been dying to go to, yet you never get to do so because you can't find anyone to go with you ... Learn to realize that it is okay to be seen by yourself in public' (p. 20). Well, the advice seems simple and straightforward, and the recommendations easy to obey. What if, however, you find them not working as well as you expected and your own doings have proved insufficient? – 'Is there anything that can be done for you' if you are willing to speak to someone else about your feeling? Yes, there fortunately is. There are therapists. And there are medications, which the therapist can prescribe (pp. 26–7).

Just like all other varieties of imperfect selves, the by-loneliness-afflicted selves, as Arlie Russell Hochschild would have put it,[16] are now advised/recommended/ forced to be 'outsourced'. What is left to our own allegedly all-powerful self, mighty enough to be able to transform feelings, is to stifle that degrading feeling of shame – and so to attend unaccompanied, despite all adverse odds, that newly opened restaurant or a cool concert.

Not much more has been left in our life-toolboxes. In the era of fast food and mobile phones, the old-fashioned skills of socializing are either forgotten or rapidly rusting due to insufficient practice. The arts of negotiating public recognition and approval of the identities of our personal choices and public endorsement of self-esteem are equally fast falling into disrepair – courtesy of surfing, the present-day substitute for walking, swimming, diving and fathoming. Reliance on the authority of verdicts pronounced by 'important others' is no longer on the cards at a time when the others tend to disappear from view and touch well before they manage to become important and we have the opportunity to acknowledge the infallibility of their judgement. Cooper seems to admit that much, though neglecting to trace the roots of that trouble and the damage it does: 'The person can be a friend, a family member, or even [sic!] a lover, but they don't *seem* [that damned feeling again!] to enrich your life the way they should' (p. 22, italics added) – and they 'seem' to do so even less to a narcissist, burdened in addition with self-inflicted loneliness. The sole company commended to the lonely self is such as has been made accessible through purchases made on the counsellors-and-therapists market.

The goods obtainable on that market are expected to arm their buyers for battles waged on two fronts. The help is sought (as the counsellors and therapists offering their services recommend) in dealing with two challenges with which the gathering tide of narcissist self-concern and self-referentiality confronts our contemporaries. The first challenge is the need to stop at least a few inches short from the threshold at which the commended narcissist stance of 'rational selfishness' turns from an asset into a liability, from praiseworthy 'norm' into condemnable perversion; from the line behind which one's own narcissist inclinations – incited as they are, day in, day out, by the breakdown of human bonds, but fed, beefed up and daily reinforced by the combined efforts of markets and media – threaten to make a budding, aspiring and up-and-coming narcissist repellent to other humans, reducing thereby to nil his chances of entering (not to mention tying up) a meaningful (let alone rewarding and gratifying) relationship with others. As specimens of that first category of help on offer, look, for instance, into Ted Dawson's *Selfishness and Self Absorption: How to Stop It from Ruining Your Relationships*, or Carol Franklin's *Narcissism: The Narcissist Laid Bare*.

The second challenge derives from coming to be cast on the receiving end of narcissist excesses; an example of responses to this challenge can be found in Eva Delano's brochure under the telling-it-all title *Narcissism Problem Solution: What to Do if Your Partner, Parent, Friend or Work Colleague is a Narcissist?* Let me warn you, however, that the borderline between the two categories of expert advice is anything but clear and solid. By the nature of their object, the counsellors and therapists are bound, in response to their clients'/patients' demands, to veer awkwardly and uneasily between two apparently contradictory demands focused on the same phenomenon: how to be an efficacious narcissus, and how to despoil a narcissus of her/his efficacy.

*

Much public attention – in Sweden, on which it has been focused, but also far beyond the Swedish borders – is currently being attracted by Eric Gandini's recent documentary film *The Swedish Theory of Love*.[17] The author points out, emphatically, that the Swedish society 'is wealthy and what that wealth offers us is free time. We can devote it to self-development and reflection.' But he adds right away that, if we look more closely, we'll discover that what, in that spectacle of happiness and well-being, comes to the fore is loneliness. In Stockholm, 58 per cent of residents dwell in one-person households, one resident in four dies in solitude, whereas the consumption of anti-depressants rose in the last twenty years by 25 per cent.

Tony Jeton Selimi's study entitled *Loneliness: The Virus of the Modern Age*[18] has the following opinion from Dr John Demartini (according to Wikipedia,[19] 'the author of nine internationally best selling published titles translated into 28 different languages') printed across the top of the front cover: 'A balm for the restless soul yearning for connection, freedom and love in the desert of emptiness', followed by no less than 30–odd expressions of acclamation and vociferous laudations signed by reputable academics and practitioners of coaching and therapy. *Loneliness: The Virus of the Modern Age* is indeed as serious a study as it is widely read and influential (Selimi in his own CV presents himself as being 'internationally known as a human behaviour and cognition expert to business leaders, CEOs, and entrepreneurs'). In his own words, Selimi dedicates his book 'to those souls who have felt the pain of being rejected or separated and felt different from what the perceived norm might be' (p. xvii).

The subject-matter of Selimi's book is a phenomenon all too well known to us from our daily experience – and by all of us resented, while paradoxically (or not so paradoxically, after all) sustained and kept going by our keen daily contributions. As he puts it in his introduction,

> separation, isolation, loneliness, and disconnection follow you in every sphere of your life. On your daily commute to work as well as in airports or restaurants, you'll see people glued to their mobile phones, iPads, tablets, computers, and laptops in desperate attempts to connect, communicate and be heard. Yet if you look around, you will see many people ignoring the presence of others right next to them, failing to create a personal connection with them, and shying away from simple conversation. (p. xxx)

At first glance, there is nothing to subtract from, and nothing to add to, such a paragraph – concise, yet managing all the same to be both informative and alerting. But what can be forgiven in the case of a paragraph can't be commuted in the case of a book. Once you've gone through, page by page, hoping eventually to muster the complete information, together with some briefing on how to go about a reasonable response to the alert and where to look for it, you are likely to feel that quite a lot needs to be added, as the most important things remain unsaid. What was meant to be an *introduction* to the theme signalled by the title of the book looks now rather like a *diversion* from the intended and promised trail.

Back in the early years of the twentieth century, the at that time frequent outbreaks of typhoid fever used to be treated by medical practitioners, who diagnosed the disease by the symptom of a very high (40 °C or even more) temperature in the afflicted bodies, by throwing the sick into a tub-full of cold water. Similar to that sort of logic is the above-sketched procedure deployed in diagnosing and treating social maladies and complaints. It is similar also in the degree of its effectiveness – obviously alive, well and gallant, and fully and truly at home, when commissioned to the job of 'outsourcing/insourcing responsibility' for which the grey area of the interface between social science and personal counselling is currently notorious. The diagnosis, semiotics and proposed treatment of loneliness, that 'virus of the modern age', are among many proofs of that logic's survival.

*

Loneliness and fear of loneliness are not just widespread *feelings*, but hard *facts* of our time firmly grounded in liquid-modern life experience; but so is the aversion and antipathy to what might have been a radical vaccine for keeping them at a distance, or even a one-off antidote against their stealthy toxins: a similarly radical solution preventing their long-term, and particularly indefinite, commitments. In view of the kind of life conditions that ooze an air of transience and unreservedly put on display their markedly temporary status, all long-term planning, even if grounded in ostensibly binding contracts of reciprocal commitment, commands little trust; if anything, it would expand (if tried) the realm of risks, by adding considerably to the number of unknown variables in every calculation of gains and losses and probabilities of success or defeat. By questioning the reliability of any company and reducing any alliance to an *ad hoc* status, networks, confederations or collusions would most certainly stop fairly short of chasing away the phantom of loneliness. That phantom hovers over every level of human togetherness – from top to bottom – stripping any kind of currently enjoyed and relished inter-human bonds, however laboriously built, of purveying reassurance of the habitat's durability.

Let's start from the bottommost, most basic and fundamental[20] level of human togetherness – that of a love partnership or 'the moral party of two'. The story of its current plight, as told by the remarkable Belgian psychoanalyst Paul Verhaeghe,[21] starts from an insight into the present condition of the household – its average and still prevailing (though with fast-thawing numerical advantage) site. 'A world has disappeared', Verhaeghe notes, 'that can be epitomised by the ubiquitous use of quotation marks – the "lady of the house" invited the husband of her "best friend" to her flat "to have a drink". Today, nothing means what it once meant . . . family life had changed drastically, the couple of yesterday has almost vanished.' He continues, following up the consequences (or causes?) of that vanishing: 'Old-fashioned declarations of romantic love – if they are still heard – sound rather hollow. The former expectations of undying love no longer apply; it is just "for a little while", "so long as it lasts". The younger generation rarely uses expressions like "my love", let alone "my husband/wife" – it has to be "my partner"' (p. 1).

The present-day condition of 'love relationships' bears all the marks of the transitoriness of interim arrangements; it is anything but straightforward and unambiguous. But, paradoxically, 'life-long loving relationship is still what both young and old are dreaming of. The failure to achieve it in reality serves only to make the dream ever more vivid' (p. 2). A decisive step towards unpacking that paradox's mystery is realizing that 'while the main thing [in a durable love relationship] used to be sex, the emphasis is now on security. *Love is a remedy in a time of loneliness*' (italics added).

Love, I'd suggest, has now become one of the pawns in the unending 'security vs freedom' game played by the human condition, with the active and dedicated, sometimes enthusiastic and some other times resentful, involvement of all of us, life's practitioners – its staple or side products and its builders, its authors and actors. The security-bent 'clearly defined limits leaving no room for doubt' (to use Verhaeghe's terms) 'were removed in the second half of the twentieth century' – that time of felling the walls and the walls falling – to open the gates to freedom of 'a new and enlightened relationship between men and women'. High expectations, rising in that hurly-burly but frustratingly brief period to the creaking accompaniment of the noise of crumbling walls, started, however, to wilt and fade once an empty space had been revealed on the other side of the walls, where it was hoped, anticipated and keenly desired that a dense mass of real answers to quandaries were to be found, unravelled, absorbed and put to a use that would be as much pleasurable as gratifying.

Love being reluctant to fill the vacant office of security provider for the swelling army of loners, and so far resistant to the efforts to lift it to the level that office demands, the escape from the stalemate in which freedom and security are embroiled is not at the moment in sight. What one promotes, the other contests. Urges for security and freedom are finely balanced, and the cross-purposed drive for more security and desire for more freedom appear now, more than ever, theoretically irreconcilable – while in practice expropriating one another, simultaneously, of their magnetism and power to act and deliver. A concurrent rise in both is all but inconceivable, whereas a rise in just one only would surely add to the aggressiveness of the other's defiance as its main effect. As far as the impact that this contest exerts on the fate of loneliness is concerned, the putting of one's wager on heads or tails coming on top feels much like making a choice between the devil and the deep blue sea.

*

Melissa Broder's both bodily and spiritual striptease[22] has turned a bestseller overnight, in both – online and offline – universes between which we daily drift and ramble, and into which our mode of being-in-the-world and our worldview, which cross-fertilize our autopsy of our selves, are split. Literary critics and the reading public this time saw eye-to-eye (not too-frequent an occurrence): the latter found in Broder's public confession what the former promised they would find: an answer to the haunting question of how to dress their own *Erlebnisse* in words which the readers desperately scouted for while labouring to encase their inward and outward sensations in a wrapping which would make them intelligible to themselves and communicable to others. The *Elle* of 14 March 2016 enthused about 'Twitter's reigning queen of angst, insecurity, sexual obsession, and existential terror via her alter ego': 'she doesn't seem to be out to shock, but to survive'. In the words of Roxane Gay, 'these essays are sad and uncomfortable and their own kind of gorgeous. They reveal so much about what it is to live in this world, right now.'

The dilemma confronting Broder's avid and (most certainly) grateful readers is accosted by the author point blank in the very first pages: 'An external attribution exists to make you feel shitty. It's a handy tool, wherein you perceive anything positive that happens to you as a mistake, subjective, and/or never a result of your own goodness. Negative things, alternately, are the objective truth. And they are always your own fault' (pp. 1–2).

Given that being born casts you inevitably and definitely in such a world – a world whose inhabitants are faced with the unappealing task of composing their real selves out of 'external attributions' – no wonder that the first statement, and simultaneously the anticipatory conclusion of the rest of the book, is: 'Bringing a child into the world without its consent seems unethical. Leaving the womb just seems insane. The womb is nirvana.' Even less bizarre – indeed, sounding rather like a foregone conclusion – is Melissa Broder's supposition, 'I didn't want to leave the womb' – as well as her emphatic, categorical admission: 'I've been trying to get back there ever since.' Why? Because 'day one on earth I discovered how to not be enough' – and that discovery continues to gain, instead of losing, in its awesomeness, day in, day out.

That womb to which Melissa Broder dreams of returning is, as she says, a specimen of nirvana. In Buddhism, from where the concept of nirvana derives, it refers to the *extinguishing* of cravings, appetites, lusts and yearnings, alongside nuisances, annoyances, naggings and harassments – indeed, 'blowing out' (as one blows out a candle) of *all* stimuli and all passions, whether positive or negative, pleasurable or painful, gratifying or discomforting. The promised result is, again in Buddhist teaching, the state of 'ego-lessness': the total opposite of Broder's state of being forever 'not enough' – constantly pursuing and never attaining, Tantalus-style, the obstreperously and infuriatingly eliding moment of arrival; and, obviously, a total reversal of the life that we, free-choosers-by-the-decree-of-fate, are bound to pursue. The yearning to 'return to the womb' and thereby re-enter the state of nirvana is the individualized loner's version of the nostalgia for the Paradise irreversibly, and so, hopelessly, lost that haunted Adam and Eve's successors. The craving for an instant and radical, in-one-fell-swoop, feat to put paid to the fatigue gestated by the unshared responsibility for one's own faux-pas, blunders and misdemeanours, cannot but reach, time and again, a magnitude grand enough to dwarf the price-tag attached to the surrender of free choice.

When it comes to dreams, nostalgia and longing for a world different from the one all-too-painfully familiar from daily autopsy, and cleansed of its all-too-tediously familiar vexations (indeed, dreams of nothing less than an alternative existential condition), they all signpost the itinerary of our collective search for a better life: a life of more comfort and less inconvenience, offering goods that the present, here-and-now world fails to deliver, and sparing the ills with which it overflows. Broder's womb/nirvana seems to be doing the job of signposting the site we've arrived at as a result of our modern historical adventure. The mediaeval Cockaigne signposted the launch of that adventure: 'Imagine a dreamland where roasted pigs wander about with knives in their backs to make carving easy, where grilled geese fly directly into one's mouth, where cooked fish jump out of the water and land at one's feet. The weather is always mild, the wine flows freely, sex is readily available, and all people enjoy eternal youth.'

This is how Herman Pleij, the University of Amsterdam's Emeritus Professor of Dutch Literature, reconstructed, in his eye-opening study[23] *Dreaming of Cockaigne*, the 'medieval peasant's dream, offering relief from backbreaking labor and the daily struggle for meager food';[24] the dream of a world of freedom and of plenty, where all the restrictions of society are 'defied (abbots beaten by their monks), sexual liberty is open (nuns flipped over to show their bottoms), and food is plentiful (skies that rain cheeses)'. This dream, I suggest, threw wide open the gateway to modern adventure, and thereafter – from the wings of the historical stage – prompted it, nudged it and kept it moving throughout its trajectory, bringing it thereby (even if stealthily and inadvertently) to clearing the site for the grand entry of the womb/nirvana: the liquid-modern precariat's dream, offering relief from the mindbending triple quandary of sustainable self-identification, of making more choices to repair the harms done by the previously taken options, and of using them both as the building materials from which to construct the meaning (meanings?) of life. The vision of Cockaigne was a call to start moving; the visualizing of the nirvana of the womb is a cry to rest.

The vision of Cockaigne used to be a utopia made to the measure of the scarcity and incapacitation suffered by people in the misery of dearth. The back-to-the-womb nirvana is the utopia made to the measure of exhilarating, while onerously taxing, over-abundance: of chances, options, choices, tempting sensations, pleasurable attractions, possible moves – and of the gambling risks of defeat that each of them is overfilled with; to the measure of people who are bound to suffer them all and who are for that reason disenchanted of enchantments, fatigued, haggard and worn out – people daunted and dispirited by what they've found in Cockaigne coming horrifyingly and soberingly close to fulfilment.

*

As if restating/summarizing the long line of arguments triggered by George Herbert Mead's analysis of the 'I' vs 'Me' dialectics, Umberto Eco[25] declares 'having the other inside one's self' to be the 'fundamental condition' of being human:

> It is his look that defines and forms us. Just as we cannot live without eating or sleeping, we cannot understand who we are without the look and response of the other. Even those who kill, rape, rob, or oppress do this in exceptional moments, but they spend the rest of their lives soliciting their fellows' approval, love, respect, and praise . . . the result of living in a community in which everyone had decided systematically never to look at us, treating us as if we did not exist, would be madness or death.

The alternative is, in Eco's words, 'a sort of bestial and solitary Adam, who still knows nothing of sexual relations, the pleasures of dialogue, love for his offspring, or the pain of losing a loved one'. And as Aristotle observed already two and a half millennia ago, only angels or beasts can live outside the *polis* – that is, outside other humans' company. Humans are neither angels nor likely to accept being beasts. Being human without human company is, purely and simply, a contradiction in terms.

Human company is the toughest and most stubborn of realities that make a living being human. Humans are neither created, nor conceivable, for a solitary existence. But there are no *other* human beings inside the nirvana of the womb (and for that reason *no humans at all*; to say 'how wonderful (warm, cosy, tranquil) it feels to be here, inside', a fully fledged human is needed – a being whose training and becoming begins only once the womb has already been left behind), whereas Cockaigne's co-residents, having their bellies constantly filled to the brim without any effort on their part, and being stripped thereby of having to perform obligatory and urgent life-tasks, would see not much need, and have little if any opportunity, to make eye contact and shake hands with others. And so the warmth of nirvana needs a sojourn in the cold and windy world for it to be appreciated and dreamt of, and the Cockaigne bliss of a lulling-to-sleep *dolce far niente* (sweet, carefree idleness) would lose (or never acquire in the first place) much of its lustre and magnetic power without the daily drudgery of spotting imminent nuisances and distresses, and efforts to nip them in the bud, to fight them back and to repair the damage they have left behind.

Under present existential conditions, the 'back to the womb' phenomenon owes its seductive attractiveness to the added drudgery prompted by both the loudly proclaimed and covertly, stealthily perpetuated 'subsidi-arization' of life's tasks, together with the responsibilities for their proper, normatively regulated fulfilment, from both the *Gemeinschaft* and the *Gesellschaft* (in Ferdinand Tönnies' terminology) or *communitas* and *societas* (in Victor Turner's rendition) sectors/aspects of human togetherness being placed upon the individual's shoulders, most of whom are notorious for being (or soon to reveal themselves to be) neither resourceful nor skilful enough to carry them to the individual agents' own satisfaction or that of those around them – judging, approving or condemning their efforts. This is another case of a yawning discrepancy between the grandiosity of tasks and the scantiness of accessible means: individuals perpetually and irredeemably over-burdened with duties that grossly transcend their carrying capacity. No wonder that the supressed memories of the womb and vague fantasies of Cockaigne are shaken from their nap by the 'storm irresistibly propelling' the actors in the liquid-modern world away from this kind of future. It is easy to guess wherefrom they are hurrying to escape, and to acquit them of any guilt for such an urge. But whereto are they – most of us – running?

The liquid-modern society of consumerist markets and individual consumers may be seen as a contraption for keeping the dream of Cockaigne alive: it makes it irresistibly tempting by bringing it within sight and seemingly close to reach through transplanting it from the realm of fantasy onto the field of all but realistic prospects, while (by perpetually raising the crossbars in the highjumps of desire) prudently stopping short of bringing the chase to a conclusion, thereby making further efforts redundant. Equipped now, in addition, with virtual reality gestated by the universally and ubiquitously accessible and constantly ready-to-serve gear of digital technology, this society may, and does, deploy a similar strategy to keep alive and render eerily realistic dreams of returning to the womb.

The womb tends to be a lonely place – but also one that is secure, unchallenged and uninterfered-with –

with no competitors vying to impair the stature of its sole resident or steal its bonuses and privileges. Were that resident – the embryo – in possession of a mind to think, self-referentiality would come to it as a matter of course: this resident of the womb would be the obvious, unchallenged and uncontested, self-evident object of the sum-total of its own concerns, scrutiny and axiological interests. As Deborah Lupton observes,[26] the introduction of digital technologies facilitates (as a matter of fact, puts in everybody's hands) 'monitoring, measuring and recording elements of one's body and life as a form of self-improvement or self-reflection' (p. 1) – the activities, let me add, in which the hypothetical embryo endowed with consciousness would be, full-time, undisturbed and uninterrupted, engaged; it would do it without being commanded or otherwise pressed, without its self-tracking having been 'encouraged, or even enforced, on people, predominantly so that the objectives of others are met' (p. 3). There are no 'others' inside the womb, our hypothetical embryo's total universe, and so the self-tracking can't be enforced and encouragement is redundant. It is the people whom that embryo would eventually join that are now, as Lupton repeatedly insists, 'frequently encouraged, "nudged", obliged or coerced into monitoring aspects of their lives so as to produce personal data that can then also be used for the purposes of others' (pp. 3–4): 'Self-tracking may be theorized as a practice of selfhood that conforms to cultural expectations concerning self-awareness, reflection and taking responsibility for managing, governing oneself and improving one's life chances. Self-tracking therefore represents the apotheosis of the neoliberal entrepreneurial citizen ideal' (p. 68).

Moreover, that 'neoliberal entrepreneurial ideal', the cultural all-but-'must' under neoliberal rule, goes an impressively long way towards explaining the appearance of the 'back to the womb' phenomenon. The latter is the product of successful socialization into the presently hegemonic philosophy of life. Like all stories of successful socialization, this one starts by recycling 'I must' into 'I will', and reaches completion by dissolving and assimilating the first in the second and making the 'must' no longer appear to be such – and to be all but invisible. In rare cases, it has been noted, it is viewed with approval, as a catapult, rather than – with resentment – as a cage. All socialization aims ultimately at conditioning people to do willingly what they have to do.

Frank Bruni sums up[27] flawlessly the condition to which we have been pushed and at which we have – gladly and thankfully – arrived:

> Those who've been raising alarms about Facebook are right: Almost every minute that we spend on our smartphones and tablets and laptops, thumbing through favorite websites and scrolling through personalized feeds, we're pointed towards a foregone conclusion. We're pressured to conform.
>
> But unseen puppet masters on Mark Zuckerberg's payroll aren't to blame. We're all real culprits. When it comes to elevating one perspective above all others and herding people into culturally and ideologically inflexible tribes, nothing that Facebook does to us comes close to what we do to ourselves.

We are pressured to conform, and we yearn to be pressured. Being guided puts paid to the fears of losing our way. Familiarity consoles and tranquillizes – or, rather, keeps us at a safe distance from situations calling for consolation and tranquillization. Myself, I used the terms 'comfort zone', 'echo chamber' and 'hall of mirrors' to denote the fenced-off mini-universe which we tend to seek, and in which we eagerly maneouvre ourselves, aided and abetted by Frank Bruni's 'unseen puppet masters on Mark Zuckerberg's payroll'. Free from disturbing and off-putting cacophony, the 'Comfort zone' is a place in which the only sounds you hear are the echoes of the noises you make and the only sights you see are the reflections of your own likeness; it is as close to the nirvana of the womb as electronic contraptions can – and do, with our assistance – bring us. In the virtual world of the online, the Internet is our smart vehicle equipped with mighty engines whose awesome power we try as much as we can to supplement and magnify even further by applying ourselves vigorously to our oars.

Bruni quotes Jonathan Haidt, the author of *The Righteous Mind* (2012): 'One of the things we want is to spend more time with people who think like us and less with people who are different.' And the Internet operators are all too keen to oblige: the Internet, Bruni points out, is 'designed to give us more of the same, whatever that same is' – and yet, more importantly, I would add, to board us off from the different, whatever that different is.

I endorse Bruni's off-putting conclusion: 'The proliferation of cable television networks and growth of the Internet promised to expand our worlds, not shrink them. Instead they've enhanced the speed and thoroughness with which we retreat into enclaves of the like-minded.'

The 'back to tribes' and 'back to the womb' phenomena, two powerful tributaries to the forceful 'back to Hobbes' current, originate from much the same source: the scare of the future embedded in the exasperatingly capricious and uncertain present. They peter out at the same tangle of blind alleys. I believe that there is little chance of their grinding to a halt unless we can stem the source from which they flow. That is, except by enticing, or forcing, the Angel of History to turn around once more.

Epilogue:
Looking Forward,
For a Change

So here we are: the denizens of an age of disruptions and discrepancies, a kind of age in which everything – or almost – may happen, while nothing – or almost – can be undertaken with self-assurance and with certainty of seeing it through; an age of causes pursuing their effects and effects tracing their causes with a minimal and constantly shrinking degree of success; an age of apparently tested means squandering (or being depleted of) their usefulness at an accelerating pace, while the search for their replacements seldom manages to reach beyond the drawing-boards stage – its achievements being no more impressive than those of the hunt after the remnants of the Malaysian Airlines Flight 370.

And so this is also an age of persistent instrumental crises. In addition to (or, more precisely, on top of) the crisis caused by the separation and near-divorce of power and politics (that is, by the falling apart of the principal among the necessary conditions of effective action, as powers emancipate from political control while politics is haunted by an interminable shortage of power), there is another instrumental crisis rapidly rising to the fore of the contemporary – and, in all likelihood, prospective – troubles: worries about institutionalized incapacity and instrumental indolence. What I have in mind is the incongruity noted by the late Ulrich Beck: of having already been cast in an advanced *cosmopolitan condition* (a universal, planet-wide interdependence, interaction and interchange) coinciding with a *cosmopolitan awareness* (not to mention cosmopolitan consciousness) as yet not much beyond the phase of birth pangs.

In order to characterize our present condition, William Fielding Ogburn would have resorted to the term 'cultural lag', which he coined in 1922 to describe the plight of the 'savages' exposed to an intense externally pressed 'modernization' of their life conditions, but still blissfully (though to their own detriment) innocent of the modern mindset and behavioural code. There is a rider perhaps, however: where, if at all, are to be found the present-day equivalents of the 'already modern' mind diagnosing the 'not-yet-modern' condition as a case of 'lagging behind', with a prospect of helping the delayed to level up with those ahead of them? More to the point, and more apposite to the task of grasping the present plight, is to recall Karl Marx finding us, the people who make history, doing it, as a rule, under conditions not of our making: 'Man makes his own history, but he does not make it out of the whole cloth; he does not make it out of conditions chosen by himself, but out of such as he finds close at hand.'[1]

Living in such an age renders the ambience of uneasiness, confusion and anxiety all but a foregone conclusion. Such an ambience makes life anything but pleasurable, soothing and gratifying. True, consumer markets offer a wide assortment of tranquillizers, antidepressants and anti-all-and-any-psychic-disorder drugs, promising and delivering a temporary – pleasurable and soothing – mitigation of psychological afflictions; these drugs are, however, intended for personal (and internal) use and not for applying to extra- or super-personal realities, and so when consumed they help to blind humans to the nature of their plight instead of contributing to the eradication of the roots of the trouble.

Once we have recalled that much about the current state of our collective condition and affairs, we are entitled to ask: how have we arrived here?

One way of presenting the history of the genus *Homo sapiens* since a small group of its members crossed, at some time between 200,000 and 150,000 BC, from Africa to the Near East, from where they would start the long and arduous process of conquering and populating the rest of the globe, is to tell its story as successive raisings of the level of societal integration. The 'primitive horde' of hunters/gatherers of those times could count no more than roughly 150 members in its ranks – as food could be provided for no more than that number of proto-humans living 'from hand to mouth' by game hunting and fruit-and-nut-picking on a territory small enough to be trodden on foot in a day. With the invention of agriculture – tillage and husbandry – and so also of food storage, humans could integrate in more numerous groups; their size rose over millennia and centuries in parallel to improvements in tools and weapons, growing efficiency of labour and rising speed of transportation. With each successive extension, the contents of the 'we' category swelled yet further, juxtaposed to 'them' – the rest of humankind, close or distant, but summarily assigned to the category of strangers – aliens, outlanders, foreigners: 'NOT us', in short – and all too often stereotyped as our actual or potential enemies.

Models of stable associations and of more or less durable coalitions between them varied between historical eras and regions of the planet, but the feature they all shared thus far was the mechanism of their inception, constitution and reproduction: the dialectics of association and dissociation, unification and separation, integration and division. Units to be integrated needed first to be separated from 'us'. In the binary opposition between 'us' (= these who are destined, bound, and so obliged to will earnestly to integrate) and 'them' (= those who are *others* to the core and beyond redemption, destined and perhaps also determined to stay forever off-limits to integration, and for those reasons needing to be barred from crossing over), 'they' played, as a rule, the role of the prior – in the terminology of structuralist semiotics, 'un-marked' – member; deciding and declaring who the people 'unlike us' are must have *preceded* the decision and declaration of who 'us' are; identification of 'them' was a necessary (and in numerous cases sufficient) condition of 'our' self-identification – and its explicit legitimation.

Equipped with this toolbox and no other, Europe entered the modern era of nation-state-building to deploy the precept of integration-through-separation in the construction of territorially sovereign modern states. Two dates deserve to be recorded as crucial for that development: 1555 and 1648. In 1555, emissaries of the ruling dynasties of Europe gathered in Augsburg to jointly deliberate on the formula that could put an end to the unbearably protracted, gory and devastating civil wars – reciprocal and repetitive massacres between Catholics and Protestants. The formula was coined: *cuius regio, eius religio* (in loose, somewhat frivolous, yet essence-grasping translation: 'He who rules decides which God his subjects worship'). It took, however, almost a century more (until 1648) – with, in the meantime, another thirty-year-long Reformation vs Counter-Reformation war, a series of epidemics and uncounted thousands more victims of both – for the envoys to travel once more, this time to Münster and Osnabrück, and manage to put their signatures to the settlement that made the Augsburg principle simultaneously legitimate to deploy and obligatory to follow for the kings and princes of participating dynasties. In practice, implementation of the said principle boiled down to the mutual territorial separation of the worshippers of the two religions-at-war, and to putting the choice between worships in the hands of the territorial sovereigns. It was in their power to privilege one of the contesting churches and discriminate against the other, and it was left to their discretion how far (if at all) they can and will tolerate the refusal of submission to the ruling faith by those among their subjects who've refused conversion.

Two centuries to the dot after the Augsburg gathering came the triple (an earthquake followed by fire and completed by a tsunami) destruction of Lisbon, at that time one of the wealthiest and most prominent European seats of culture, arts and trade. To the most eminent minds of the Enlightenment, it gave an opportunity to rethink, re-evaluate and reposition the wisdom of Divine design in the order of things. In *Poème sur le désastre de Lisbonne* Voltaire charged Nature, the principal among God's creations, with demonstrating in Lisbon its true face of moral indifference and criminal injustice ('l'innocent, ainsi que le coupable, subit également ce mal inévitable') and proving thereby its total unfitness to secure victory of good over evil unless taken under human control. *Deus*, so went the corollary to that verdict, having finished his labour of creation, became *absconditus*; the world needed to be taken under new – this time human – management.

That message took time to sink into the new hegemonic philosophy, human minds and attitudes. The Lisbon disaster and its aftermath took place in the context of the ascendant absolutist monarchy, and the message of *les philosophes* was originally unpacked as a call addressed to fellow philosophers together with their mighty and supposedly omnipotent patrons, to enlighten the law-making decisions of the absolute monarchs of the day (assumed to hold virtually unlimited authority and capability to change human reality by decree), so they could secure the triumph of good over evil which the dumb and numb Nature failed to deliver, let alone to make secure.

Two centuries after Münster and Osnabrück, however, from the 1848 'Spring of Nations' onwards, the formula *cuius regio, eius religio*, was wedded to the transfer of *regio* from prospectively enlightened monarchs to *le peuple*, newly enfranchised – and, in this novel version, deployed in the service of nation, state, and nation-state building. Courtesy of the European imperial/colonialist adventure, the revised formula, together with its applications, were transplanted on the other continents, and, at the Versailles Peace Conference in 1919–21, proclaimed by its Chairman, and the US President, Woodrow Wilson (in the form of the 'Right of Nations to Self-determination') as a universal principle of the worldwide human cohabitation.

How to reconcile globalization/cosmopolitanization of finances, industry, trade, knowledge and communication and the indisputable globality of the survival problems humanity faces with endemic locality and self-referentiality of the political instruments which Wilson's principle calls to manage all those crucial ingredients of the human condition? This is the hardest of all the quandaries that humanity faces – indeed, the meta-quandary on which the resolution of all the lesser, derivative dilemmas will ultimately depend. There is a yawning gap between what *needs* to, and what *can*, be done; between what matters and what counts to the makers; between what happens and what is desirable; between the size of the problems humanity faces and the reach and capacity of the tools available to manage them. As Benjamin Barber, supported by a wide and expanding company of observers, insists: the nation-state, the thus far ultimate entity in the long chain of integrated systems capable of concerted collective action, has acquitted itself more or less decently of the task of serving the cause of independence and autonomy for whose performance it was designed and adjusted, but is demonstrating daily its singular unfitness to act effectively under the present condition of planet-wide interdependence of humans. A large number of yet more adamantine and iconoclastic onlookers hurry to write (grossly exaggerated, as Mark Twain would have quipped) obituaries of the deceased, or about-to-expire, nation-states era.

Until now, all successive enlargings of the scale of

integrated political units to a higher and more inclu-
sive (and, by necessity, more abstract, imagined, remote
from the reach of our senses) level followed, by and
large, the expanding capacity of accessible means of
communication and the ensuing expansion of the realm
of possibilities. Each step on that road ushered in a new
set of options, and so also set the stage for new replays
of the sometimes inflamed, but perpetually smouldering,
conflict between mutually antagonistic – defensive and
offensive, conservative and progressive, forward- and
backward-heeding – attitudinal syndromes. The feature
which all those steps up to that point shared was, however, the renegotiation of the 'us vs them' division and
the intimate link between redrawing the boundaries of
integration with realigning the frontlines of separation.

Here lies the fully and truly unprecedented novelty of
the challenge posited by the next lifting of the human
level of integration presently on the agenda – and the
until now un-confronted and un-dealt-with obstacle to
the raising of collective consciousness, in tandem with
the conduct it inspires and legitimizes, to the already
attained level of our interdependence and interaction (or,
to recall the legacy of Ulrich Beck's teaching, comple-
menting the cosmopolitan situation with cosmopolitan
awareness). In stark opposition to all previous (ultimately successful) battles to raise the scope of integration
to a higher level, this one – the ascent of integration to
the level of humanity as a whole – *can't deploy either
the 'appointment of a shared enemy' weapon or the 'us
against them' device*, previously tested and believed to
be indispensable conditions of victory. The postulated
'cosmopolitan awareness' has thrown-open doors and
a standing invitation to join as its defining traits; its

coming of age is tantamount to the abandonment of the 'enemy' and the 'once a stranger, forever a stranger' ideas, those foundations of the 'us vs them' division. And so the challenge of the moment consists in nothing less than designing – for the first time in human history – integration without separation to rest on. So far, there are few if any signs that this challenge is likely to be met head-on and soon. As Samuel P. Huntington pointedly summed up the present-day tendencies, in the post-Cold War world, 'people are discovering new but often old identities and marching under new but often old flags which lead to wars with new but often old enemies'.[2] He supports that opinion by quoting, from a Michael Dibdin novel, the 'one grim *Weltanschauung* . . . well expressed by the Venetian nationalist demagogue':

> There can be no true friends without true enemies. Unless we hate what we are not, we cannot love what we are. These are the old truths we are painfully rediscovering after a century and more of sentimental cant. Those who deny them deny their family, their heritage, their culture, their birthright, their very selves. They will not lightly be forgiven.[3]

The 'Venetian nationalist demagogue' imagined by Dibdin is a certain Ferdinando Dal Maschio, a founder of the 'Lega Veneta' movement and advocate of the Nuova Repubblica Veneta, ruled from Venice, being cut out of and away from the Italian Republic – one of the relics of 'sentimental cant'; he is a figure in sharp conflict even with the real-world figure of Umberto Bossi, notorious for demanding that a similar operation be committed on an independent Padania to be ruled from Milan, whom he sees as insufficiently radical and unfit to be classified among 'friends' ('We Venetians must take control of our own destiny . . . For over a century we have let ourselves be beguiled by the chimera of nationalism [first the Austrian Empire and then Italy ruled from Rome]. Now there are those who urge us to deliver ourselves meekly into the power of Milan').

The quotations above come from the public harangues of Dal Maschio the demagogue. The following are extracts from the intimate confessions of Dal Maschio the home-baked thinker and theorist: 'The centre can't hold any longer . . . The periphery is where the action is. In the new Europe, the periphery *is* the centre. It's time to come home. Time to come back to your roots, back to what is real and meaningful and enduring'; 'The new Europe will be no place for rootless drifters and cosmopolitans with no sense of belonging. It will be full of frontiers, both physical and ideological, and they will be rigorously patrolled. You will have to be able to produce your papers or suffer the consequences.'

This may feel like a grim *Weltanschauung* indeed, but it is one fast mustering a large and expanding congregation; it won't be a gross exaggeration to announce it as the forthcoming hegemonic philosophy that puts fissiparousness in the room about to be vacated by the near-defunct nation-state integration, and the 'back to the roots' drive in the still empty room furnished to accommodate the yet-unborn cosmopolitically integrated humanity.

Huntington's own – no less grim – *Weltanschauung* chimes well with the image of the 'new Europe' as painted by dal Muschio and bound to be approved by the demagogues of countries united by their shared distaste for all things tolerant and democratic and particularly those of the liberally tolerant family – as well as to be admired and applauded by the swelling crowds of their converts and recruits. Huntington suggests that 'culture and cultural identities' will, from now on, be 'shaping the patterns of cohesion, disintegration and conflict in the post-Cold War world'. In that world, 'the most important distinctions between peoples are not ideological, political, or economic. They are cultural':

> People define themselves in terms of ancestry, religion, language, history, values, customs and institutions. They identify with cultural groups: tribes, ethnic groups, religious communities, nations ... People use politics not just to advance their interests but also to define their identity. We know who we are only when we know who we are not and often only when we know whom we are against. (pp. 20–1)

This rule, Huntington suggests, is not just a particular and transient contingency of the moment: 'People are always tempted to define people into us and them, in-group and the other, our civilization and those barbarians.' Whether they always surrender, and really cannot but surrender, to the above temptation remains a moot question, and a question that, in all probability, will always be possible to answer merely *retrospectively* – in reference to what has already happened, excluding from view the future, notorious as it is for its unpredictability and its penchant for taking even the greatest minds by surprise and catching them unprepared. But Huntington's anticipation of the post-Cold War departures have been thus far amply confirmed, while the trends current at the moment I am writing these words seem to make the future supply of further proofs for his forebodings all but a foregone conclusion.

The big question is whether the temptations spotted by Huntington may be rejected – and if so, then on what conditions? In other words, can the birth of 'cosmopolitically integrated humanity' be induced and the newborn safely delivered?

The most convincing response (even though it is anything but a magic spell claiming to produce its results instantly, inviting us instead to undertake a protracted, tortuous effort by no means guaranteed to succeed) to this seminal, live-or-die question for humanity, I found in an address by Pope Francis – currently the one person among public figures with considerable planet-wide authority who is sufficiently bold and determined to raise and tackle this sort of questions – given on 6 May 2016 when he received the European Charlemagne Prize. That answer is: *the capacity for dialogue*, and here I quote it verbatim as it should be learned:

> If there is one word that we should never tire of repeating, it is this: dialogue. We are called to promote a culture of dialogue by every possible means and thus to rebuild the fabric of society. The culture of dialogue entails a true apprenticeship and a discipline that enables us to view others as valid dialogue partners, to respect the foreigner, the immigrant and people from different cultures as worthy of being listened to. Today we urgently need to engage all the members of society in building 'a culture which privileges dialogue as a form of encounter' and in creating 'a means for building consensus and agreement while seeking the goal of a just, responsive and inclusive society' (Evangelii Gaudium, 239). Peace will be lasting in the measure that we arm our children with the weapons of dialogue, that we teach them to fight the good fight of encounter and negotiation. In this

way, we will bequeath to them a culture capable of devising strategies of life, not death, and of inclusion, not exclusion. This culture of dialogue should be an integral part of the education imparted in our schools, cutting across disciplinary lines and helping to give young people the tools needed to settle conflicts differently than we are accustomed to do. Today we urgently need to build 'coalitions' that are not only military and economic, but cultural, educational, philosophical and religious. Coalitions that can make clear that, behind many conflicts, there is often in play the power of economic groups. Coalitions capable of defending people from being exploited for improper ends. Let us arm our people with the culture of dialogue and encounter.

Dialogue, with all that it entails, reminds us that no one can remain a mere onlooker or bystander. Everyone, from the smallest to the greatest, has an active role to play in the creation of an integrated and reconciled society. This culture of dialogue can come about only if all of us take part in planning and building it. The present situation does not permit anyone to stand by and watch other people's struggles. On the contrary, it is a forceful summons to personal and social responsibility.

This address, sent to 'all of us', as all of us need 'to take part in planning and building' the culture of dialogue capable of healing the wounds of our multicultural, multicentred and multiconflictual world, is first and foremost directed to us *hoi polloi*, and in no way constrained for the use of professional politicians claiming (and expected to master) expertise in the art of negotiation. The intention behind Pope Francis' message is to bring the fate of peaceful cohabitation, solidarity and collaborations between humans from the fuzzy and obscure realm of high politics 'as seen on TV' down to the street, workshops, offices, schools and public spaces where we, the rank-and-file *hoi polloi*, meet and converse; to take the issue, fate and hope of humanity's integration out of the hands of the troop commanders in Samuel Huntington's *Clash of Civilizations* – and put it into the care of the day-in, day-out encounters of neighbours and workmates, in which we all participate and appear to each other as caring or callous parents, faithful or disloyal partners, helpful or ungenerous neighbours, pleasurable or tedious companions – instead of in the garb of representatives or specimens of mutually alien civilizations, traditions, religious faiths or ethnicities.

For this to happen, however, some additional conditions need to be met for us to perceive and treat each other as 'valid dialogue partners'. The chances of fruitful dialogue, as Pope Francis reminds us, depend on our reciprocal respect and assumed, granted and mutually recognized equality of status:

> The just distribution of the fruits of the earth and human labour is not mere philanthropy. It is a moral obligation. If we want to rethink our society, we need to create dignified and well-paying jobs, especially for our young people. To do so requires coming up with new, more inclusive and equitable economic models, aimed not at serving the few, but at benefiting ordinary people and society as a whole. This calls for moving from a liquid economy to a social economy.

There are no shortcuts leading to a quick, adroit and effortless damming of the 'back to' currents – whether to Hobbes, to tribes, to inequality or to the womb. I repeat: the present task of lifting human integration to the level of all humanity is likely to prove unprecedentedly arduous, onerous and troublesome to see through and complete. We need to brace ourselves for a long period marked by more questions than answers and more problems than solutions, as well as for acting in the shadow of finely balanced chances of success and defeat. But in this one case – in opposition to the cases to which Margaret Thatcher used to impute it – the verdict 'there is no alternative' will hold fast, with no likelihood of appeal. More than at any other time, we – human inhabitants of the Earth – are in the either/or situation: we face joining either hands, or common graves.

Notes

Introduction: The Age of Nostalgia

1 In Svetlana Boym, *The Future of Nostalgia*, Basic Books 2001.

2 Franz Kafka, 'The Departure', in *The Collected Short Stories of Franz Kafka*, ed. Nahum N. Glatzer, Penguin 1988, p. 449 (trans. Tania and James Stern).

3 https://mail.aol.com/webmail-std/en-gb/DisplayMessage?ws_popup=true&ws_suite=true.

4 Boym, *The Future of Nostalgia*, p. xvi.

5 E. H. Carr, *What is History?*, first published by Cambridge University Press in 1961.

6 See http://howitreallywas.typepad.com/how_it_really_was/2005/10/wie_es_eigentli_1.html.

7 Peter Drucker, *The New Realities*, Butterworth-Heinemann Ltd 1989.

1 Back to Hobbes?

1 Timothy Snyder, *Black Earth: The Holocaust as History and Warning*, The Bodley Head 2015, p. 320.

2 Leo Strauss, *Natural Right and History*, University of Chicago Press 1965 [1950].

3 See https://thisishell.com/guests/henry-giroux.

4 Max M. Mutschler, 'On the Road to Liquid Warfare?', BICC Working Paper, 2016.

5 In *The Arms Bazaar: Shattered Lives*, Control Arms Campaign, October 2003, ch. 4, p. 54. Here quoted from www.globalissues.org/article/74/the-arms-tra de-is-big-business#Asworldtradeglobalizessodoes thetradeinarms.

6 www.theguardian.com/news/datablog/2012/mar/02/ arms-sales-top-100–producers.

7 *Small Arms Survey*; see https://www.amnesty.org/ en/latest/news/2015/08/killer-facts-the-scale-of-the-global-arms-trade.

8 See Georg Simmel, 'Fashion', *American Journal of Sociology*, 62, May 1957 – http://sites.middlebury. edu/individualandthesociety/files/2010/09/Simmel. fashion.pdf.

9 See Gabriel Tarde, *Law of Imitation*, H. Holt and Co. 1903 (trans. Elsie Clew Parsons) (French original published in 1890).

10 Elihu Katz et al., *Echoes of Gabriel Tarde: What We Know Better or Different 100 Years Later*, USC Annenberg Press, 2014.

11 This statement – sounding rather banal in this rendering – is commonly ascribed to the pioneer of pragmatist philosophy, William James, although the paraphrase is in fact a few steps removed from his assertion (in Lecture II in his book *What is Pragmatism?*: 'There can be no difference anywhere that doesn't MAKE a difference elsewhere.' In the same lecture, James traces his assertion to Charles

Peirce's statement, made first in his article 'How to Make our Ideas Clear', published in the January 1878 issue of *Popular Science Monthly*: 'Our beliefs are really rules for action . . . To develop a thought's meaning, we need only determine what conduct it is fitted to produce' – an idea that led Ludwig Wittgenstein to define understanding as knowing how to go on. See also http://theblogofciceronianus.blogspot.co.uk/2013/11/differences-that-make-no-difference.html.

12 Thompson, *Media and Modernity: A Social Theory of the Media*, Polity 1995.

13 Jock Young, *The Exclusive Society*, Sage 1999, pp. 8–9.

14 Jock Young, *The Vertigo of Late Modernity*, Sage 2007, p. 54.

15 Cf. Willem Schinkel, 'The Will to Violence', *Theoretical Criminology*, 8/1, February 2004. See also https://www.ncjrs.gov/App/publications/abstract.aspx?ID=206082.

16 Umberto Eco, *Il cimitero di Praga*, 1st Italian edition 2010; here quoted from Richard Dixon's English translation, Vintage Books 2012.

17 Umberto Eco, *Serendipities: Language and Lunacy*, Phoenix 1998 (trans. William Weaver).

18 Stanley Cohen, *Visions of Social Control*, Polity 1985, p. 125.

19 For a most brilliant presentation of this case, read J. G. Ballard, *Kingdom Come*, Fourth Estate 2014.

20 www.socialeurope.eu/2011/08/the-london-riots-on-consumerism-coming-home-to-roost.

21 www.nytimes.com/2016/01/20/opinion/rethinking-

college-admissions.html?emc=edit_ty_20160120&
nl=opinion&nlid=43773237&_r=0.
22 www.nytimes.com/2016/01/22/opinion/the-anxietie
s-of-impotence.html?emc=edit_th_20160122&nl=to
daysheadlines&nlid=43773237&_r=0.

2 Back to Tribes

1 Michael Walzer, *Spheres of Justice: A Defence of Pluralism and Equality*, Basic Books 1983, p. 38.
2 Bruce Rozenblit, *Us Against Them: How Tribalism Affects the Way We Think*, Transcendent Publications 2008, pp. 74–5.
3 Ibid., p. 54.
4 Luc Boltanski, 'Sociologie et critique sociale: dérive ou renouveau?', in Luc Boltanski and Nancy Fraser, *Domination et émancipation: pour un renouveau de la critique sociale*, Grand Débats 2014, p. 64.
5 Celia de Anca, *Beyond Tribalism; Managing Identities in a Diverse World*, Palgrave Macmillan 2012, pp. xxii–xxvi.
6 Quoted from Karl Marx, *The Eighteenth Brumaire of Louis Bonaparte*, the American 1897 translation reprinted in the UK by Amazon 2008, pp. 1–2. Also https://www.marxists.org/archive/marx/works/1852/18th-brumaire/cho1.htm.
7 David Lowenthal, *The Heritage Crusade and the Spoils of History*, Viking 1997, p. ix.
8 Ibid., pp. 5–6.
9 Ernest Gellner, *Nations and Nationalism*, Blackwell 1983, pp. 1, 4.
10 Umberto Eco, *Faith in Fakes: Travels in Hyperreality*, Vintage 1995.

11 See George Lakoff, *The All New Don't Think of an Elephant*, Chelsea Green Publishing 2014.

12 See Friedrich Nietzsche, *Aphorisms on Love and Hate*, Penguin Classics 2015, pp. 21, 29–30.

13 www.nytimes.com/2016/03/11/opinion/campaign-stops/what-are-trump-fans-really-afraid-to-say.html?emc=edit_th_20160311&nl=todaysheadlines&nlid=43773237&_r=0.

14 http://printfriendly.com/print/?url=https%3A%2F%2Fwww.socialeurope.eu%2.

15 www.independent.co.uk/voices/donald-trump-is-just-the-kind-of-president-america-needs-a6924986.html.

16 Lakoff *The All New Don't Think of an Elephant*, pp. 108–9.

17 Ibid., pp. xi–xii.

18 Anthony D. Smith, *Nations and Nationalism in a Global Era*, Polity 2007, pp. 51–2.

19 Fredrik Barth, *Ethnic Groups and Boundaries: The Social Organization of Culture Difference*, Waveland Press 1998, p. 10.

20 Hobsbawm, *Nations and Nationalism since 1780: Programme, Myth, Reality*, Cambridge University Press 2016, p. 163.

21 As Karl Marx memorably put it (in the earlier quotation from *The Eighteenth Brumaire of Louis Bonaparte*): 'Men make their own history, but they do not make it as they please; they do not make it under self-selected circumstances, but under circumstances existing already, given and transmitted from the past.'

22 Here quoted from the French translation, *La question des nationalités et la*

social-démocratie, Guérin Littérature 1987. The two principles spelled out above were suggested by Bauer as a means to secure, simultaneously, continuity of national identities and lasting (and hopefully peaceful) cooperation between them inside a multiethnic Austro-Hungarian state, with its irreducible 'mélange de nations' – see particularly pp. 250, 364ff.
23 Hobsbawm, *Nations and Nationalism since 1780*, p. 175.
24 Michel Agier, *Le couloir des exilés: être étranger dans un monde commun*, Éditions du Croquant 2011, p. 95.
25 See www.nytimes.com/2016/01/15/opinion/fermisi natra-dimaggio-and-capone-american-immigration. html.
26 See www.nytimes.com/2016/01/08/opinion/a-shame ful-round-up-of-refugees.html?/emc=ed.

3 Back to Inequality
1 Benjamin Disraeli, *Sybil, Or the Two Nations*, Oxford University Press 1998, p. 66.
2 http://usatoday30.usatoday.com/news/opinion/col umnist/raasch/2004-07-28-raasch_x.htm.
3 https://en.wikipedia.org/wiki/Two_Americas#Exter nal_links.
4 See http://mrzine.monthlyreview.org/2010/kalecki22 0510.html.
5 The essay was roughly based on the lecture given to the Marshall Society in Cambridge in the spring of 1942.
6 He warned, however – prophetically – that the 'capitalist bosses' would be up in arms against such a

gross interference by the governments with the very foundations of their domination:

> the maintenance of full employment would cause social and political changes which would give a new impetus to the opposition of the business leaders. Indeed, under a regime of permanent full employment, the 'sack' would cease to play its role as a 'disciplinary measure'. The social position of the boss would be undermined, and the self-assurance and class-consciousness of the working class would grow . . . 'Discipline in the factories' and 'political stability' are more appreciated than profits by business leaders. Their class instinct tells them that lasting full employment is unsound from their point of view, and that unemployment is an integral part of the 'normal' capitalist system.

7 http://nymag.com/daily/intelligencer/2016/03.
8 See Vic George and Roger Lawson (eds.), *Poverty and Inequality in Common Market Countries*, Routledge & Kegan Paul 1980, p. 241.
9 Frank Parkin, *Marxism and Class Theory*, Tavistock 1979, p. 83.
10 Robert L. Heilbroner, *Business Civilization in Decline*, W. W. Norton 1976, p. 109.
11 Robert K. Merton, 'Social Structure and Anomie', *American Sociological Review*, 3, 1938, 672–82.
12 Walter Garrison Runciman, *Relative Deprivation and Social Justice: A Study of Attitudes to Social Inequality in Twentieth-century England*, University of California Press 1966.
13 Barrington Moore Jr, *Injustice: The Social Bases of Obedience and Revolt*, M. E. Sharpe 1978.
14 https://www.boundless.com/sociology/textbooks/bo

undless-sociology-textbook/social-change-21/social-movements-140/relative-deprivation-approach-771-1936.

15 Leonard Riessmann, 'Levels of Aspiration and Social Class', *American Sociological Review*, 18, 1953, 233–43.

16 J. C. Davies, 'The J-Curve of Rising and Declining Satisfactions as a Cause of Some Great Revolutions and a Contained Rebellion', in *Violence in America: Historical and Comparative Perspectives*, ed. Hugh Davis Graham and Ted Robert Gurr, Praeger 1969, pp. 690–730.

17 Paul Verhaeghe, 'Neoliberalism Has Brought Out the Worst in Us', *The Guardian* 23 April 2016; see www.thedailycall.org/?p=86957.

18 www.nytimes.com/2016/04/24/business/economy/velvet-rope-economy.html?emc=edit_th_20160424&nl=todaysheadlines&nlid=43773237&_r=0.

19 Zygmunt Bauman, *Does the Richness of the Few Benefit Us All?*, Polity 2013.

20 Daniel Raventós, *Basic Income: The Material Conditions of Freedom*, Pluto Press 2007 (trans. from Spanish by Julie Wark), p. 8. Raventós' definition does not depart far from Phillip van Parijs' earlier – and by many considered the still fundamental – definition of UBI:

> An income paid by a government, at a uniform level and at regular intervals, to each adult member of society. The grant is paid, and its level is fixed, irrespective of whether the person is rich or poor, lives alone or with others, is willing to work or not. In most versions – certainly in mine – it is granted not only to citizens,

but to all permanent residents. (*What's Wrong with a Free Lunch?*, Beacon Press 2001, p. 5)

Van Parijs selects Karl Marx and Joseph Charlier, both under the influence of Charles Fourier, as original (both in 1848) pioneers of the idea. And let me add that, to whomever the palm for inventing the 'universal basic income' idea is eventually awarded, the fact will remain that, still in April 2016, when his review of Bregman's *Utopia for Realists* was published (see www.opendemocracy.net/Neil.Howard/utopia-for-realists-review), Neil Howard could express his amazement with 'Free money for everyone. It sounds mad' – only to add a few lines later, 'But one of Bregman's great strengths is to present his ideas and the evidence for them in such a way as to make them sound not only not mad but in fact downright sensible', and to conclude the extensive review on the tone of highest praise: 'It is fabulously well-researched and engagingly well-written. It's also extremely accessible. One of Bregman's real qualities is to write about the revolutionary as if it were run-of-the-mill.'

21 www.theguardian.com/comments are free/2015/feb/01/paying-everyone-a-basic-income-would-kill-off-low-paid-menial-jobs.
22 Rutger Bregman, 'Cutting out the Middleman', *The Economist*, 4 November 2010.
23 www.oecd.org/dev/pgd/46240619.pdf.
24 http://jama.jamanetwork.com/article.aspx?articleid=197482.
25 Van Parijs, *What's Wrong with a Free Lunch?*, p. 14.
26 Ibid., p. 111.

4 Back to the Womb

1 http://bostonreview.net/us-books-ideas/ronald-aronson-privatization-hope.

2 A term introduced by Louis Althusser (in 'Ideology and Ideological State Apparatuses (Notes towards an Investigation)', in *Lenin and Philosophy and Other Essays*, Verso 1970, to denote the 'hailing' of a person by invoking her/his preconceived, assumed/imposed, categorial assignment. Both those who are hailed and those who hail them are ideologically trained to recognize in the act of 'interpellation' the reference to their status and mutual relationship.

3 https://www.ted.com/talks/tim_jackson_s_econo mic_reality_check/transcript?language=en.

4 Umberto Eco, 'How Not to Use the Cellular Phone', in *How to Travel with Salmon and Other Essays*, Mariner Books 1995 (trans. William Weaver).

5 Steve Fraser, *The Age of Acquiescence*, Little, Brown and Company 2015.

6 Christopher Lasch, *The Culture of Narcissism: American Life in An Age of Diminishing Expectations*, Warner Books 1979.

7 Anthony Elliott, *Concepts of the Self*, 2nd edition, revised and updated, Polity 2007, p. 85.

8 See Sigmund Freud, *On Narcissism: An Introduction*, Read Books 2013 [1914].

9 Rutger Bregman, *Utopia for Realists: The Case for a Universal Basic Income, Open Borders, and a 15-hour Workweek*, The Correspondent 2016, pp. 22–3.

10 Ibid., p. 25.

11 Cederström Spicer and André Spicer, *The Wellness Syndrome*, Polity 2015, p. 3.

12 Steven Poole, *You Aren't What You Eat*, London 2012.

13 https://en.wikipedia.org/wiki/Ayn_Rand#Popular_interest.

14 See Ayn Rand, *The Virtues of Selfishness*, A Signet Book by Penguin, which has sold 1.3 million copies since its publication in 1964.

15 Wilson Cooper, *Love Yourself – Your Life Depends on It: How to Transform your Life and Overcome the Loneliness*, 2015, p. 7.

16 See Arlie Russell Hochschild, *The Outsourced Self: Intimate Life in Market Times*, Henry Holt and Company 2012. Outsourcing to hired experts of 'those services that reach into the heart of our emotional lives, a realm previously more shielded from the market', is in Hochschild's view 'the greatest innovation of the contemporary scene'. The pattern previously tested on safety razors, self-winding watches or fast food proved to be handy when a new potentially profitable market of loneliness suffered by an unstoppably growing number of humans lined up for a site where they could outsource the trouble they didn't know how to tackle.

17 http://weekend.gazeta.pl/weekend/1,150913,2006 4106,sztokholm-europejska-stolica-samotnych-jak-szwedzi-stali.html.

18 Selimi, *Loneliness: The Virus of the Modern Age*, Balboa Press 2016.

19 https://en.wikipedia.org/wiki/John_Frederick_Demartini.

20 See my essay 'Morality Begins at Home: Or the Rocky Road to Justice', in Zygmunt Bauman, *Postmodernity and Its Discontents*, Polity 1997.

21 See Paul Verhaeghe, *Love in a Time of Loneliness: Three Essays on Drive and Desire*, Karnac Books Ltd 2011 (trans. Plym Peters and Tony Langham).

22 Melissa Broder, *So Sad Today*, Scribe 2016.

23 Herman Pleij, *Dreaming of Cockaigne: Medieval Fantasies of the Perfect Life*, Columbia University Press 2001 (trans. Diane Webb). See also http://cup. columbia.edu/book/dreaming-of-cockaigne/9780 231117029.

24 https://en.wikipedia.org/wiki/Cockaigne.

25 See Eco, 'When the Others Appear on the Scene' – a letter to Cardinal Carlo Maria Martini, in *Five Moral Pieces*, Vintage 2001 (trans. Alastair McEwen).

26 Deborah Lupton, *The Quantified Self*, Polity 2016.

27 Frank Bruni, 'How Facebook Warps Our World', *New York Times*, 22 May 2016; http://nyti.ms/1s1hq1G.

Epilogue: Looking Forward, for a Change

1 www.gutenberg.org/files/1346/1346-h/1346-h. htm.

2 Samuel P. Huntington, *The Clash of Civilizations, and the Remaking of World Order*, Free Press 1997, p. 20.

3 Michael Dibdin, *Dead Lagoon*, here quoted from the Kindle version of the Faber & Faber 2012 edition.